Official

SQA
Past Papers
WITH ANSWERS

Higher
Computing
2010–2014

HODDER
GIBSON
AN HACHETTE UK COMPANY

Hodder Gibson is grateful to the copyright holders, as credited on the final page of the Question Section, for permission to use their material. Every effort has been made to trace the copyright holders and to obtain their permission for the use of copyright material. Hodder Gibson will be happy to receive information allowing us to rectify any error or omission in future editions.

Hachette UK's policy is to use papers that are natural, renewable and recyclable products and made from wood grown in sustainable forests. The logging and manufacturing processes are expected to conform to the environmental regulations of the country of origin.

Orders: please contact Bookpoint Ltd, 130 Park Drive, Abingdon, Oxon OX14 4SE. Telephone: (44) 01235 827720. Fax: (44) 01235 400454.

Lines are open 9.00–5.00, Monday to Saturday, with a 24-hour message answering service. Visit our website at www.hoddereducation.co.uk. Hodder Gibson can be contacted direct on: Tel: 0141 848 1609; Fax: 0141 889 6315; email: hoddergibson@hodder.co.uk

This collection first published in 2014 by

Hodder Gibson, an imprint of Hodder Education,

An Hachette UK Company

2a Christie Street

Paisley PA1 1NB

{BrightRED   Hodder Gibson is grateful to Bright Red Publishing Ltd for collaborative work in preparation of this book and all SQA Past Paper, National 5 and Higher for CfE Model Paper titles 2014.

Typeset by PDQ Digital Media Solutions Ltd, Bungay, Suffolk NR35 1BY

Printed in the UK

A catalogue record for this title is available from the British Library

ISBN 978-1-4718-3679-4

3 2 1

2015 2014

Introduction

Study Skills – what you need to know to pass exams!

Pause for thought

Many students might skip quickly through a page like this. After all, we all know how to revise. Do you really though?

Think about this:

"IF YOU ALWAYS DO WHAT YOU ALWAYS DO, YOU WILL ALWAYS GET WHAT YOU HAVE ALWAYS GOT."

Do you like the grades you get? Do you want to do better? If you get full marks in your assessment, then that's great! Change nothing! This section is just to help you get that little bit better than you already are.

There are two main parts to the advice on offer here. The first part highlights fairly obvious things but which are also very important. The second part makes suggestions about revision that you might not have thought about but which WILL help you.

Part 1

DOH! It's so obvious but …

Start revising in good time

Don't leave it until the last minute – this will make you panic.

Make a revision timetable that sets out work time AND play time.

Sleep and eat!

Obvious really, and very helpful. Avoid arguments or stressful things too – even games that wind you up. You need to be fit, awake and focused!

Know your place!

Make sure you know exactly **WHEN and WHERE** your exams are.

Know your enemy!

Make sure you know what to expect in the exam.

How is the paper structured?

How much time is there for each question?

What types of question are involved?

Which topics seem to come up time and time again?

Which topics are your strongest and which are your weakest?

Are all topics compulsory or are there choices?

Learn by DOING!

There is no substitute for past papers and practice papers – they are simply essential! Tackling this collection of papers and answers is exactly the right thing to be doing as your exams approach.

Part 2

People learn in different ways. Some like low light, some bright. Some like early morning, some like evening / night. Some prefer warm, some prefer cold. But everyone uses their BRAIN and the brain works when it is active. Passive learning – sitting gazing at notes – is the most INEFFICIENT way to learn anything. Below you will find tips and ideas for making your revision more effective and maybe even more enjoyable. What follows gets your brain active, and active learning works!

Activity 1 – Stop and review

Step 1

When you have done no more than 5 minutes of revision reading STOP!

Step 2

Write a heading in your own words which sums up the topic you have been revising.

Step 3

Write a summary of what you have revised in no more than two sentences. Don't fool yourself by saying, "I know it, but I cannot put it into words". That just means you don't know it well enough. If you cannot write your summary, revise that section again, knowing that you must write a summary at the end of it. Many of you will have notebooks full of blue/black ink writing. Many of the pages will not be especially attractive or memorable so try to liven them up a bit with colour as you are reviewing and rewriting. **This is a great memory aid, and memory is the most important thing.**

Activity 2 — Use technology!

Why should everything be written down? Have you thought about "mental" maps, diagrams, cartoons and colour to help you learn? And rather than write down notes, why not record your revision material?

What about having a text message revision session with friends? Keep in touch with them to find out how and what they are revising and share ideas and questions.

Why not make a video diary where you tell the camera what you are doing, what you think you have learned and what you still have to do? No one has to see or hear it, but the process of having to organise your thoughts in a formal way to explain something is a very important learning practice.

Be sure to make use of electronic files. You could begin to summarise your class notes. Your typing might be slow, but it will get faster and the typed notes will be easier to read than the scribbles in your class notes. Try to add different fonts and colours to make your work stand out. You can easily Google relevant pictures, cartoons and diagrams which you can copy and paste to make your work more attractive and **MEMORABLE**.

Activity 3 – This is it. Do this and you will know lots!

Step 1

In this task you must be very honest with yourself! Find the SQA syllabus for your subject (www.sqa.org.uk). Look at how it is broken down into main topics called MANDATORY knowledge. That means stuff you MUST know.

Step 2

BEFORE you do ANY revision on this topic, write a list of everything that you already know about the subject. It might be quite a long list but you only need to write it once. It shows you all the information that is already in your long-term memory so you know what parts you do not need to revise!

Step 3

Pick a chapter or section from your book or revision notes. Choose a fairly large section or a whole chapter to get the most out of this activity.

With a buddy, use Skype, Facetime, Twitter or any other communication you have, to play the game "If this is the answer, what is the question?". For example, if you are revising Geography and the answer you provide is "meander", your buddy would have to make up a question like "What is the word that describes a feature of a river where it flows slowly and bends often from side to side?".

Make up 10 "answers" based on the content of the chapter or section you are using. Give this to your buddy to solve while you solve theirs.

Step 4

Construct a wordsearch of at least 10 X 10 squares. You can make it as big as you like but keep it realistic. Work together with a group of friends. Many apps allow you to make wordsearch puzzles online. The words and phrases can go in any direction and phrases can be split. Your puzzle must only contain facts linked to the topic you are revising. Your task is to find 10 bits of information to hide in your puzzle, but you must not repeat information that you used in Step 3. DO NOT show where the words are. Fill up empty squares with random letters. Remember to keep a note of where your answers are hidden but do not show your friends. When you have a complete puzzle, exchange it with a friend to solve each other's puzzle.

Step 5

Now make up 10 questions (not "answers" this time) based on the same chapter used in the previous two tasks. Again, you must find NEW information that you have not yet used. Now it's getting hard to find that new information! Again, give your questions to a friend to answer.

Step 6

As you have been doing the puzzles, your brain has been actively searching for new information. Now write a NEW LIST that contains only the new information you have discovered when doing the puzzles. Your new list is the one to look at repeatedly for short bursts over the next few days. Try to remember more and more of it without looking at it. After a few days, you should be able to add words from your second list to your first list as you increase the information in your long-term memory.

FINALLY! Be inspired...

Make a list of different revision ideas and beside each one write **THINGS I HAVE** tried, **THINGS I WILL** try and **THINGS I MIGHT** try. Don't be scared of trying something new.

And remember – "FAIL TO PREPARE AND PREPARE TO FAIL!"

Higher Computing

The course

Homework, NAB tests and prelim exams will have given you some idea of how you will be assessed. Completing the coursework task, which you do in class, means that you will have up to 60 marks under your belt before the exam even starts.

The course is split into two core units and one optional unit (from a choice of three topics). The two core topics are Computer Systems and Software Development. They are examined in Sections I and II of the exam with Section III covering the optional topic.

Section I

The first section of the exam contains 30 marks drawn equally from the two core topics. They are short response questions, similar in level of difficulty to the type of questions you met in your NAB tests, but are not multiple choice.

Section II

There are 60 marks available in Section II, again drawn equally from the two core topics. Each question is built around a central theme or scenario and is generally worth about ten to fifteen marks. The opening paragraph, or stem, of each question may contain information vital to a successful answer. Your answers will generally be short paragraphs. Learn the set piece questions, e.g. systems calculations or the pseudocode for the standard algorithms.

Section III

The third section has 50 marks and consists of extended response questions from each optional unit. Each of these questions is built around a central theme or scenario, with a stem containing important information and focussing more on problem solving.

The exam

Knowledge and Understanding and Problem Solving

In the exam, Knowledge and Understanding questions test recall of facts and understanding of concepts, such as:

- Name the two people involved in the analysis stage.
- Describe one method of detecting virus activity.

Problem Solving questions ask you to apply your knowledge in context, such as:

- Describe the additional hardware and software that Miss Batra will need to carry out this task.
- Explain why a vector graphic package is not suitable in this situation.
- Calculate the size of the uncompressed sound file that will be stored.

When you finish a question, read quickly over your answer and try to think like an examiner.

Every year candidates lose marks for silly errors such as:

- Missing out parts of questions – even whole pages.
- Misreading questions and failing to hit the points needed.
- Writing down everything they know, even if it has nothing to do with the question, and contradicting themselves.

- Not including an appropriate level of technical detail in answers or failing to use the correct terminology (there is a reason that a list of required terms is published by the SQA).
- Poor layout, which is really important in calculations.
- Missing out steps in calculations, not rounding the answer and not writing down the units.
- Not including a quick sketch or diagram (if it helps).

This book of past papers is a valuable resource. It will help you to spot key themes, practise common questions and gauge what should be in the perfect answer.

General advice

Good preparation is vital! Going into an exam without preparing in advance will cost you vital marks before you even pick up your pen. Below are a few tips that will help you.

- Get a copy of the SQA content grids from your teacher, or get them on the SQA website. Use red to highlight the parts of the grid you have never heard of, green for the stuff you know really well and yellow for the topics that you are a bit unsure of. This "traffic light" technique can help give your revision focus.
- Make up a glossary of key terms – this is really useful for learning technical Computing jargon. List the words you are supposed to know, together with their meanings in your own words. This will improve your chances of learning them and being able to remember them in an exam.
- Make your own notes and use a good revision guide. Compile flashcards with facts or frequently asked questions on them. Try mind mapping and diagrams to help you visually structure knowledge.
- Read the past papers and the marking instructions carefully. This is where the clues to what the examiners are looking for are to be found. Good answers contain an appropriate amount of technical detail and include the context where asked for.
- Read the whole paper through once quickly. Make sure you know which optional topic you are doing. You have about a minute per mark for Higher Computing. Section I should take about 30 minutes and you should be onto Section III after about an hour and a half.
- Take account of how many marks each question is worth and shape your answer to match. The wording of questions can also give you a clue.
  - o "state" questions only need a short sentence or phrase to gain each of the marks.
  - o "describe" questions need more detailed sentences. Bullet points are useful if you have trouble with longer answers. One bullet per mark!
  - o Answers to "explain" questions have two parts – a cause and an effect. An example might be "DVD-RW is not a suitable backing storage medium because it can only hold 4.7 gigabytes."

Watch for "… in this context" or "… for this situation", as at least some of the marks will depend on explicitly linking the Computing theory to the scenario of the question.

Potential questions

Typical Section I questions might be:

- *State the 8 bit twos complement representation of the number -137.*
- *Describe how FLOPs are used to measure processor performance.*
- *Describe what is meant by the iterative nature of the software development process.*
- *Name a graphical design method. Use a diagram to illustrate your answer.*

Typical questions in Section II might be:

- *Describe, referring to appropriate buses and control lines, the steps in the fetch-execute cycle.*
- *Calculate the maximum size of addressable memory in a computer with a 32 bit data bus and a 24 bit address bus.*
- *Explain why a trojan horse is not a virus.*
- *Use pseudocode to show how the name entered is found in the list of members' names.*
- *Explain why the use of parameter passing and local variables makes software more portable.*
- *Explain why an event-driven language would be more suitable for producing the training software.*

Typical questions in Section III might be:

Part A: Artificial Intelligence

- *Explain how a neural net may be trained.*
- *Describe the image acquisition and image understanding stages of computer vision.*
- *Explain what is meant by a combinatorial explosion.*
- *Use an example to explain the meaning of the terms inheritance and recursion.*
- *Use the letters on the search tree on the right to show the order of nodes visited using a depth-first and breadth-first search.*

Problem solving questions in AI often require candidates to solve queries or write rules. There is always a "trace" using Prolog-like facts and rules. Make sure that you get plenty of practice doing traces. They are a bit like logic puzzles. Make sure that you learn how to structure your answer and to use the correct terminology.

A short example of a trace on a query to find out if a violin is a musical instrument might be:

- Goal is instrument(violin)
- Match at line 8, instrument(violin) IF brass(X), subgoal brass(X), X instantiated to violin
- No matches found, subgoal fails, backtrack to line 8.
- Match at line 12, instrument(violin) IF string(X), subgoal string(X), X instantiated to violin
- Match at line 14, subgoal succeeds
- Goal succeeds. Output is "true"

Part B: Computer Networking

- *Describe the application and transport layers of the OSI model.*
- *Describe the structure of a class C IP address.*
- *Describe how the Regulation of Investigatory Powers Act affects Kathryn here.*
- *Describe two disaster avoidance strategies for a school network.*
- *Describe how firewalls and walled gardens are used to filter internet content.*
- *Explain the difference between synchronous and asynchronous data transmission.*
- *Describe how CRC is used in the error checking during data transmission.*

Problem solving questions are heavily scenario-based and your success will rely upon your ability to spot the relevant facts in the stem and other parts of the question.

Part C: Multimedia Technology

- *Explain the terms streaming and embedded files when talking about a multimedia application.*
- *Describe the function of a CCD and an ADC in the capturing of a digital image.*
- *Explain how Run Length Encoding is used to compress a bitmap graphic.*
- *State two common attributes of notes stored in MIDI format.*
- *Explain what is meant by the term convergent technologies.*

One key skill in Multimedia Technology is how to lay out calculations. There are several calculation questions to choose from, such as…

- *Calculate the size of an uncompressed 4 minute video file taken at 25 fps.*

Each frame is 512 by 500 pixels and is in 32 bit colour.

- Number of frames = Video Time (s) x Frame Rate (fps)

    = 4 x 60 x 25 = 6000 frames
- Size of one frame = pixels per frame x Colour Depth (bytes)

    = 512 x 500 x 4 = 1024000 bytes = 1000 Kb
- File Size of clip = 6000 x 1000 Kb = 5859.375 Mb = 5.72 Gb

Multimedia Technology is mainly about the application of the theory in real life contexts. Watch for the details and remember that your knowledge is expected to go beyond the Systems unit!

Good luck!

Remember that the rewards for passing Higher Computing are well worth it! Your pass will help you get the future you want for yourself. In the exam, be confident in your own ability. If you're not sure how to answer a question, trust your instincts and just give it a go anyway. Keep calm and don't panic! GOOD LUCK!

HIGHER

2010

[BLANK PAGE]

X206/301

NATIONAL QUALIFICATIONS 2010	THURSDAY, 3 JUNE 9.00 AM – 11.30 AM	COMPUTING HIGHER

Attempt **all** questions in Section I.

Attempt **all** questions in Section II.

Attempt **one** sub-section of Section III.

Part A	Artificial Intelligence	Page 10	Questions 18 to 22
Part B	Computer Networking	Page 16	Questions 23 to 26
Part C	Multimedia Technology	Page 20	Questions 27 to 31

For the sub-section chosen, attempt **all** questions.

Read all questions carefully.

Do not write on the question paper.

Write as neatly as possible.

Marks

SECTION I

Attempt all questions in this section.

1. Convert this *8-bit two's complement* binary number into a decimal.

   11010011   **1**

2. Jane is concerned about a virus infecting her computer.

   (*a*) *Watching* is one *virus code action*. Describe the term "watching".   **2**

   (*b*) State **one** other virus code action.   **1**

3. A *register* can be used to store a *memory address*. State the **two** other types of item that can be stored in a register.   **2**

4. A new printer has 640 megabytes of RAM installed. State **one** reason why the printer has RAM installed.   **1**

5. Complete the **two** missing stages of the *fetch-execute cycle*.

1	The memory address of the next instruction is placed on the address bus.
2	
3	The instruction is transferred to the processor on the data bus.
4	

   2

6. Greg buys a single copy of a popular computer game. He then makes several copies to give out to his friends.

   (*a*) State the name of the law that he has broken.   **1**

   (*b*) State **one** reason why making copies of the game is illegal.   **1**

7. Explain **one** difference between a *Local Area Network* (*LAN*) and a *Wide Area Network* (*WAN*) in terms of *transmission media*.   **2**

8. Describe **one** reason for connecting a network using a *switch* rather than a *hub*.   **2**

Marks

SECTION I (continued)

9. Most high level languages have several *data types* available.

   (a) State what is meant by a *real* variable. **1**

   (b) State the most suitable *data structure* and *data type* for storing the list called "valid" in the pseudocode shown below.

   ```
   For each member of list
     If gender(current) = "M" or gender(current) = "F" Then
       Set valid(current) to true
     Else
       Set valid(current) to false
     End If
   End fixed loop
   ```
   2

10. *Design* is the second stage of the software development process.

    (a) Explain the importance of the design stage for one of the later stages in the software development process. Your answer should refer to the name of the stage that you have chosen. **2**

    (b) Describe how *stepwise refinement* can be used to help produce a detailed design. **2**

11. Documentation is produced at **each** stage of the software development process.

    (a) Name **one** item of documentation that is produced at the *implementation stage*. **1**

    (b) One purpose of creating documentation at **each** stage is to provide a starting point for the next stage.

    State **one** other purpose of documentation. **1**

    (c) Describe the role that the programmer might play in the production of the *technical guide* during the *documentation* stage. **1**

12. Software can be evaluated in terms of *efficiency* and *portability*.

    (a) Software can be described as efficient if it does not waste memory.

    Describe **one** way of making software efficient in terms of **memory usage**. **2**

    (b) Describe what is meant by the term "portability". **2**

Marks

SECTION I (continued)

13. A sports centre has purchased software to assist with daily tasks such as bookings. The new software includes a *scripting language*.

    State **one** use of a scripting language.

    1

    (30)

[END OF SECTION I]

Marks

SECTION II

Attempt all questions in this section.

14. Carolyn uses a computer to edit photographs that she has taken with her digital camera.

   (*a*) When Carolyn switches on her computer, system software in ROM finds and loads the operating system. Name this system software in ROM. **1**

   (*b*) Carolyn transfers the photographs from her camera to her computer using a *serial interface*.

       (i) Two functions of the interface are *data format conversion* and *handling of status signals*. Describe how each of these functions would be involved in this data transfer. **2**

       (ii) State **two** other functions of an interface. **2**

   Carolyn reduces the *bit-depth* of the photographs from 24 bits to 16 bits before saving the photographs onto the hard disk of her computer system.

   (*c*)   (i) Describe **one** advantage of reducing the bit-depth of the photographs from 24 to 16. **2**

       (ii) Describe **one** disadvantage of reducing the bit-depth of the photographs from 24 to 16. **2**

       (iii) A 4 inch by 6 inch photograph with a resolution of 600 dpi and using 16-bit colour depth is stored. Calculate the file size of the photograph.

       State your answer using appropriate units. Show all your working. **3**

   (*d*) Two functions of the operating system are *memory management* and *input/output management*. Describe the roles of each of these **two** functions when a photograph is saved on to the hard drive. **2**

   (*e*) Carolyn's camera uses *solid state storage*. Explain **one** reason why solid state storage is used in digital cameras. **2**

   (*f*) Carolyn uses photo editing software that allows her to store a photograph using *JPEG* or *GIF* file format. Describe **one** difference between these two file formats. **2**

[Turn over

Marks

SECTION II (continued)

15. Ernie has bought a new computer with 24 *control lines*, a 32-bit *address bus* and a 64-bit *data bus*.

    (a) Calculate the **maximum possible** amount of memory that Ernie's computer can address.   State your answer using appropriate units.   Show all your working.   **3**

    (b) Ernie's computer has 16 megabytes of *cache* memory.   Describe how the use of cache memory may improve system performance.   **2**

    (c) Ernie requires new word processing software to use on his computer system. Describe **one** *compatibility issue* that should be considered when buying new software.   **2**

    (d) Two methods of measuring performance are *application based tests* and *MIPS*.

        (i) Explain why MIPS may be the better measure of **processor** performance than application based tests.   **2**

        (ii) State **one** other measure of processor performance.   **1**

    Ernie's computer is part of a small *peer-to-peer network* of computers in his family home.   There are three other computers in the house.

    (e) Explain **one** reason why the family created a *peer-to-peer* network instead of a *client-server* network.   **2**

Marks

SECTION II (continued)

16. Mrs Laird sets her Higher Computing class the task of writing a program that will take in three items – day, month and year. These three variables will have the same data type. The program will then output a "DateofBirth" variable with six characters, as shown below.

Input Variables		
day	month	year
15	Jun	1992

Output Variable
DateofBirth
150692

(a) State the only *data type* that the pupils can use for **all three** of the "day", "month" and "year" variables. Justify your answer. **2**

(b) Name the operation used to extract the last two characters from the contents of the "year" variable. **1**

(c) Part of the program will take the contents of **month** e.g. "Jun" and turn this into the corresponding **two** character value for that month e.g. "06". Mrs Laird tells the pupils they must **not** use IF statements to implement this part of the program.

Use pseudocode to design an algorithm for this part of the program. You should show only the first two months in your algorithm. **3**

(d) Name the operation used to join the three values together to produce the six characters for "DateofBirth". **1**

(e) The contents of the "DateofBirth" variable are to be held in memory in ASCII format. Calculate the mininum amount of memory required to store the contents of this variable. **2**

(f) The pupils are using a *procedural* language to write their programs.

(i) State **two** features of procedural languages. **2**

(ii) State **one** feature of *event-driven* languages that is **not** commonly found in procedural languages. **1**

(g) Mrs Laird tells the pupils that their programs must be easily *maintainable*. Describe **two** characteristics of a program that make it easily "maintainable". **2**

(h) Mrs Laird also tells the pupils that they must avoid the use of *global variables* in their programs where possible.

(i) State the meaning of the term "global variable". **1**

(ii) Explain why the pupils have been asked to avoid the unnecessary use of global variables when programming. **2**

[Turn over

Marks

SECTION II (continued)

17. Henry works for a company that maintains office buildings. He decides to write a program to print labels for the room keys in a new office block. The block has 38 floors, each with 25 rooms. The label will consist of the floor number and the room number. The design for the program is shown below alongside a sample section of output.

```
For each of 38 floors
    For each of 25 rooms
        Display "Floor Number:" and floor_no
        Display "Room Number:" and room_no
    Next room
    Display two blank lines
Next floor
```

Floor Number: 12
Room Number: 3
Floor Number: 12
Room Number: 4

(a) Once the program has been written it must be translated. Describe clearly why using a *compiler* to translate the code produced from **this** algorithm would be more efficient in terms of **processor usage** than using an *interpreter* to translate the same code. **2**

(b) State **one** example of how text output from a program could be *formatted*. **1**

(c) The company decide to include Henry's code as a new function in their building management software.

State the **type** of maintenance being carried out on the building management software by adding this section of code as a subprogram. **1**

(d) In order for Henry's program to operate correctly for **any** office building **two** parameters would have to be passed to it.

(i) State what these **two** parameters would be. **2**

(ii) State whether these parameters would be passed to the subprogram by *value* or by *reference*. Justify your answer. **2**

(e) Another subprogram in the building management software is used to find the range of temperatures in a building in one day. The temperature is recorded every 15 minutes within a 24 hour period and stored in a list.

Use pseudocode to design **one** algorithm to find **both** the **highest** and **lowest** temperatures in this list. **5**

(60)

[END OF SECTION II]

SECTION III

Attempt ONE sub-section of Section III

For the sub-section chosen, attempt *all* questions.

Marks

SECTION III

PART A—Artificial Intelligence

Attempt all questions.

18. Game playing is one area of research in *artificial intelligence*. Computers are being used in games such as chess and card games.

   (*a*) (i) State **one** meaning of the term "artificial intelligence".   1

   (ii) Name **one** popular test used to determine whether a computer system can be described as having artificial intelligence or not.   1

   (iii) Explain why training computer systems to play simple games is thought to be a good way of investigating artificial intelligence.   2

   (*b*) (i) One aspect of intelligence is *cognitive ability*. State **two** other aspects of intelligence that are used in game playing.   2

   (ii) Describe how **each** of your answers in part (i) may be used in game playing.   2

   (*c*) *Parallel processing* and *increased memory* have improved the performance of computers in game playing.

   (i) Describe how parallel processing can improve performance in games such as chess.   2

   (ii) Describe how increased memory can improve performance in games such as chess.   2

Marks

SECTION III

PART A—Artificial Intelligence (continued)

19. An area of artificial intelligence attempts to model systems based on the human brain. A diagram of a neuron found in the human brain is shown below.

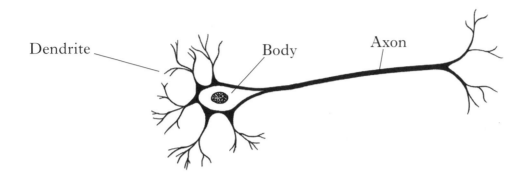

(a) Describe **one** similarity between an *artificial neuron* and a human neuron. 1

(b) State **two** changes that can take place within an *artificial neural system* during the learning (or training) process. 2

(c) In order to develop an artificial neural system a *restricted domain* should be identified.

   (i) Explain what is meant by the term "restricted domain". 1

   (ii) State **one** other characteristic of a domain suitable for implementing as an artificial neural system. 1

(d) The artificial neural system can be *hard-wired* or implemented as a *software model*.

   State **one** advantage of implementing an artificial neural system as a software model instead of being hard-wired. 2

20. A company has developed a computer vision system to monitor swimmer safety in outdoor swimming pools. The system monitors activity in the pool using a number of cameras and will alert lifeguards to potential problems.

(a) *Computer vision* consists of a number of stages.

   (i) Name and describe the **first** stage of computer vision. 2

   (ii) *Edge detection* will be used to analyse the image. Explain **one** problem for edge detection in **this** situation. 2

(b) The cameras capture still images using **65536** colours. Calculate the *bit depth* of the images captured. 1

Marks

SECTION III

PART A—Artificial Intelligence (continued)

21. A student has created software about extinct animals for a museum. The software has a *knowledge base* with information about animals and the century in which they became extinct.

```
1    extinct(dodo seventeenth)
2    extinct(sea_cow eighteenth)
3    extinct(atlas_bear nineteenth)
4    extinct(rice_rat twentieth)
5    extinct(eastern_elk nineteenth)
```
The dodo became extinct in the seventeenth century.

```
6    older(seventeenth eighteenth)
7    older(eighteenth nineteenth)
8    older(nineteenth twentieth)
```
The seventeenth century is older than the eighteenth century.

```
9    earlier(A B) IF older(A B)
```
Century A is earlier than century B if century A is older than century B.

```
10   earlier(A B) IF older(A C) AND
                    earlier(C B)
```
Century A is earlier than century B if century A is older than century C and century C is earlier than century B.

```
11   extinct_earlier(X Y) IF extinct (X A) AND
                             extinct (Y B) AND
                             earlier (A B)
```
Animal X became extinct earlier than animal Y if animal X became extinct in century A and animal Y became extinct in century B and century A is an earlier century than B.

(*a*) State the solutions to the following query:

```
? extinct(X nineteenth)
```
2

(*b*) When testing the knowledge base the student entered a query to identify the centuries that came before the twentieth century.

The solutions to the query were:

```
A = nineteenth
A = eighteenth
A = seventeenth
```

State the query that the student entered that resulted in this output.

3

Marks

SECTION III

PART A—Artificial Intelligence (continued)

21. (continued)

(c) Trace the **first** solution to the query:

```
? extinct_earlier(X sea_cow)
```

In your answer you will be given credit for the correct use of the term *sub-goal*.   6

(d) *Negation* is implemented in Prolog by the use of *NOT*. Describe the effect of *NOT* in the evaluation of a query.   1

(e) The knowledge base could have been represented using a *semantic net*.

   (i) Draw a simple semantic net of the fact at line 7.   2

  (ii) Use your diagram to explain how a semantic net is used to represent knowledge.   2

(f) The student chose to implement the software using a *declarative* language rather than a *procedural* language.

One reason for this choice was the facility to use *facts* and *rules*. State **one** other reason for choosing a declarative language.   1

[Turn over

Marks

SECTION III

PART A—Artificial Intelligence (continued)

22. A *search tree* is shown below. The *goal state* is represented by the node C.

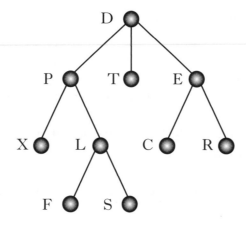

Depth-first and *breadth-first* are search techniques that may be used to find the goal state.

(a) State the order in which nodes would be visited using **depth-first**, stopping when the goal state is reached.   1

(b) (i) State **one** advantage of using **depth-first** when compared to breadth-first to search the tree.   1

   (ii) State **one** advantage of using **breadth-first** when compared to depth-first to search the tree.   1

(c) (i) State which one of these two search techniques makes use of *backtracking*.   1

   (ii) Explain how the search technique named in part (c) (i) employs backtracking when searching the tree shown above.   2

(d) The most *efficient* search would visit the nodes in the order **DEC**. This would use a *heuristic search*.

   Describe how a heuristic search finds the nodes in the path **DEC**.   3

   (50)

[END OF SECTION III—PART A]

[Turn over for Question 23 on *Page sixteen*

Marks

SECTION III

PART B—Computer Networking

Attempt all questions.

23. The manager of the Sea Bay Hotel has created a website to display details of the hotel and allow customers to make online bookings.

    She hopes that this will cut down on the number of errors in bookings, such as double-booking and employees entering the wrong details for bookings.

    (a) The web address for the Sea Bay Hotel is:

    www.seabayhotel.co.uk

    A user enters this web address into a browser. Describe how the *domain name server* uses the web address to access the website.   **3**

    (b) Online hotel booking systems may be subject to additional problems such as hacking and credit card fraud.

    Name and describe **one** other possible illegal activity that the hotel could suffer from as a result of allowing customers to book and pay online.   **2**

    (c) The hotel uses an intranet with ten computers, two printers and a scanner connected to it.

    State the most suitable class of *IP address* for this network. Justify your answer.   **2**

    (d) The manager is concerned about employees accessing unsuitable websites from the hotel's computers.

        (i) Describe how *Internet filtering software* would prevent employees from accessing unsuitable websites.   **1**

        (ii) Describe how a *walled garden* would prevent employees from accessing unsuitable websites.   **2**

    (e) Despite these precautions, the manager suspects that an employee is accessing websites containing illegal material.

    State **two software** actions that the *Regulation of Investigatory Powers Act* would allow the police to undertake.   **2**

    (f) The Sea Bay Hotel website can be found by using a *search engine*. A search engine can use either a *spider* or a *meta-search*.

    Describe how **each** of these two methods is used by a search engine.   **2**

Marks

SECTION III

PART B—Computer Networking (continued)

23. (continued)

(g) Some of the *HTML* coding for the hotel website is shown below.

```
<html>
<head>
<title><i>Sea Bay Hotel Home Page</i></title>
<body>
<center><h1>Sea Bay Hotel</h1></center>
<p>Welcome to the Sea Bay Hotel</p>
</body>
</htm>
```

Identify **two** errors that are present in the above HTML code. 2

(h) Describe **two** changes that could be made to the HTML code of the webpage to increase the number of hits by a search engine, once the above errors have been corrected. 2

(i) The manager is worried about *viruses*. *Anti-virus software* has been installed on all of the hotel computers.

Name and describe **one** class of virus that the anti-virus software might detect. 2

24. Legends is a catering company that owns 130 restaurants nationwide. Each restaurant is connected to the head office through a Wide Area Network (WAN) to allow communication and file sharing.

(a) The network uses *CSMA/CD*.

   (i) Describe how CSMA/CD operates. 4

   (ii) State **one** way in which CSMA/CD **reduces** network performance. 1

(b) The TCP/IP protocol uses *packet switching* when transmitting files over the network. Explain **one** advantage of packet switching over *circuit switching* when transmitting files over a network. 2

[Turn over

Marks

SECTION III

PART B—Computer Networking (continued)

25. Bishopsland High School has its computers connected in a Local Area Network (LAN). The network is connected using cables.

    (a) The network conforms to the *Open Systems Interconnection* (OSI) model.

    Two layers of the OSI model are the *Session layer* and the *Network layer*.

    (i) State **one** task carried out at the Session layer.   1

    (ii) Name a networking device that operates at the Network layer.   1

    (b) Data can be sent over a network using *synchronous* or *asynchronous* data transmission.

    Explain **one** advantage of synchronous compared with asynchronous data transmission.   2

    (c) A 200 megabyte file is to be downloaded at 100 megabits per second.

    Calculate how many seconds it will take to download the file. Show all working.   2

    A pupil has suggested that a wireless network would be better than the current cable network.

    (d) (i) Name a **hardware** device that must be present in a computer to enable it to connect to a wireless network.   1

    (ii) Explain the function of this device.   1

    (e) State **two** disadvantages of converting to a wireless network compared to using cables.   2

    (f) The school network has been subject to a *denial of service* attack.

    Describe **one** method of using software to carry out a denial of service attack.   1

    (g) The school is situated in a remote area that was previously considered *Information Poor*.

    (i) Describe **one** way that the pupils may now be *Information Rich*.   1

    (ii) Explain **one** social implication of the change to Information Rich.   1

Marks

SECTION III

PART B—Computer Networking (continued)

26. When data is transmitted across a network, it is important that error checking takes place.

    A *parity check* and a *cyclic redundancy check* are two methods of error checking.

    (a) Explain why a cyclic redundancy check is more effective than a parity check. 2

    (b) *Error checking* improves the **integrity** of data passing through the network.

    Explain **one** way that error checking may **reduce** the performance of the network. 2

    (c) The network must be able to avoid catastrophic failure. Describe **two** software *disaster avoidance* techniques that could be used to make the network less prone to failure. 2

    (d) If the disaster **avoidance** techniques fail, the network may crash. A *backup server* and *mirror disks* are both *backup strategies* that could be used to **recover** from this disaster.

    (i) Describe **one** benefit and **one** drawback of using a backup server as a disaster recovery strategy. 2

    (ii) Describe **one** benefit and **one** drawback of using a mirror disk as a disaster recovery strategy. 2

    (50)

[END OF SECTION III—PART B]

Marks

SECTION III

PART C—Multimedia Technology

Attempt all questions.

27. Two photographs are to be used as the basis for an animation. A digital camera is used to take the photographs.

(a) Describe in detail how an image is captured and converted into a digital format by the camera.

3

(b) Each frame in the completed 12 second animation is held as a GIF with a resolution of 640 × 480 pixels. The animation has a frame rate of 24 frames per second.

Calculate the file size of the animation before compression. State your answer using appropriate units. Show all working.

4

(c) The animation is tested on different computers and the colours displayed in the animation vary slightly.

(i) State which software technique could reduce this colour variation problem.

1

(ii) Explain how this technique reduces this colour variation problem.

2

(d) The animation files are compressed using LZW. Describe how the *LZW compression technique* compresses files.

2

Marks

SECTION III

PART C—Multimedia Technology (continued)

28. A DJ has connected a record turntable to his computer to transfer tracks from his vinyl record collection to his computer.

(a) Describe **one** function of the *sound card* **during** the transfer of the data to the computer.

1

(b) The DJ wants to store the tracks with no loss of sound quality.

State a suitable file format for storing the tracks without losing sound quality.

1

(c) Clips from several tracks are combined into a single file, but one of the clips is too quiet and another is too loud.

   (i) State the technique that should be used to solve this problem.

1

   (ii) Describe how your answer to part (i) solves the problem.

2

(d) The completed track plays for 5 minutes and is 16 bit stereo with a sampling rate of 44.1 KHz.

Calculate the uncompressed file size of this track. State your answer using appropriate units. Show all working.

3

The DJ often uses *surround sound* in his shows.

(e) Explain **one** advantage of surround sound over stereo.

2

The DJ has stored several tracks as *MIDI* files.

(f) Describe how individual notes are stored in the MIDI file format.

2

(g) Describe **one** benefit of using the MIDI file format to store tracks used with surround sound.

2

[Turn over

Marks

SECTION III

PART C—Multimedia Technology (continued)

29. The developers of a new digital video camera have to decide which communication interfaces to include in the camera.

    The video camera is to be suitable for *streaming* live video.

    (a) Explain **one** reason why a *Bluetooth* interface is unlikely to be chosen for streaming live video.   2

    (b) (i) Recommend the most suitable type of interface for this situation.   1

    (ii) Justify your choice in part (i).   2

    (c) State why it would be an advantage to have *hardware codecs* built in to the video camera rather than loading in the software.   2

30. A museum uses multimedia presentations to provide information about various exhibits.

    The software that was used to develop the presentations has a *WYSIWYG* interface.

    (a) Explain **two** reasons why WYSIWYG would help the developer during the implementation stage.   2

    All of the presentations include links to video clips. The video clips are stored in either *MPEG* or *AVI* format.

    (b) Describe how files are stored in the MPEG format.   3

    (c) AVI does not allow compression but has been chosen for some short clips that are displayed in small windows.

    Explain why the AVI format is suitable for storing these video clips.   2

    Some of the presentations are made available for downloading from the museum website.

    (d) (i) Explain why a *container file* would be used to store the presentations.   2

    (ii) Describe **one** problem that may be encountered when using a container file.   1

    To improve the display of the presentations, the museum upgrades the *graphics cards* on its computers.

    (e) Other than converting signals, state **two** ways a graphics card assists the processor when displaying graphics.   2

Marks

SECTION III

PART C—Multimedia Technology (continued)

31. The logo shown is stored as an *object oriented* graphic.

The logo appears in a variety of sizes on both printed documents and monitors.

(*a*) Describe **two** advantages of storing the graphic in *object oriented* format rather than *bitmapped* format.   2

One object in the logo is a circle. The circle is altered so that it is shown in 3D.

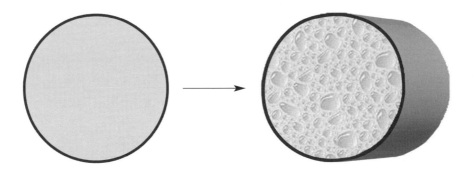

(*b*) Name **two** additional attributes that require to be stored to create the 3D representation shown.   2

(*c*) Name a suitable file format for the 3D logo.   1

(50)

[END OF SECTION III—PART C]

[END OF QUESTION PAPER]

[BLANK PAGE]

[BLANK PAGE]

X206/301

NATIONAL
QUALIFICATIONS
2011

FRIDAY, 3 JUNE
9.00 AM – 11.30 AM

COMPUTING
HIGHER

Attempt **all** questions in Section I.

Attempt **all** questions in Section II.

Attempt **one** sub-section of Section III.

Part A	Artificial Intelligence	Page 10	Questions 17 to 20
Part B	Computer Networking	Page 14	Questions 21 to 24
Part C	Multimedia Technology	Page 18	Questions 25 to 28

For the sub-section chosen, attempt **all** questions.

Read all questions carefully.

Do not write on the question paper.

Write as neatly as possible.

SA X206/301 6/7510

Marks

SECTION I

Attempt all questions in this section.

1. State the largest whole number that can be stored as a 10-bit positive integer.   **1**

2. Name and describe a method for measuring the performance of computers.   **2**

3. Data storage compensates for differences in speed between computers and peripherals. This is achieved through *buffering* and *spooling*.

   (a) Explain the difference between buffering and spooling.   **2**

   (b) Compensation for differences in speed between the computer and peripherals is one function of an *interface*. State **two** other functions of an interface.   **2**

4. (a) State the **type** of virus that may affect a computer during the start up process.   **1**

   (b) *Replication* and *camouflage* are two *virus code actions*. State **two** other virus code actions.   **2**

5. State **one** advance in computer **hardware** that has led to the increased use of computer networks.   **1**

6. (a) Describe an example in which an image stored as a vector graphic could have a larger file size than if the same image was stored in a bitmapped format.   **2**

   (b) A bitmapped graphic has a *bit-depth* of 24 bits and a *resolution* of 300 dpi.

      (i) State the number of colours that may be represented in this graphic.   **1**

      (ii) State the effect that increasing the bit-depth will have on the file size of the graphic.   **1**

7. *Analysis* is the first stage of the software development process.

   (a) Name the document produced at the end of the analysis stage.   **1**

   (b) Explain why the production of this document could be an *iterative* process.   **1**

Marks

SECTION I (continued)

8. *Pseudocode* is a design notation often used during the software development process.

    (*a*) Pseudocode should include *data flow*. State the purpose of data flow.   1

    (*b*) Other than data flow, state **two** benefits to a programmer of a design written in pseudocode.   2

9. State what is meant by the term "boolean variable".   1

10. Software is usually written using *subprograms*. Two types of subprogram are *procedures* and *functions*.

    (*a*) State how the use of subprograms increases the *maintainability* of a program.   1

    (*b*) Readability of code affects maintainability. Other than using subprograms, state **one** way to improve **readability** of code.   1

    (*c*) Explain **one** difference between a procedure and a function.   2

11. A program contains three variables, of **the same type**, with the following values:

variable1	variable2	variable3
8	4	84

    The program is written in a new language called SQAM. It contains the line of code shown below. The symbol ? represents a particular operation.

    variable3 = variable1 ? variable2

    (*a*) The value 84 is assigned to **variable3**. State the single common operation carried out by the ? symbol.   1

    (*b*) State the *data type* that must have been used for **all three** of the variables.   1

12. A *macro* can be used within application software to automate a task.

    (*a*) Name the *type* of programming language used to create macros.   1

    (*b*) Other than saving time, for example during writing or testing, state **two** further benefits of using macros.   2

    (30)

[END OF SECTION I]

Marks

SECTION II

Attempt all questions in this section.

13. Paula buys a new laptop computer which has 4 Gigabytes of *main memory* and 12 Megabytes of *cache* memory.

   (a) State **two** differences between main memory and cache memory.　　　2

   (b) The computer has a **maximum** addressable memory of 16 Gigabytes. Its *address bus* width is 32.

   　(i) Calculate the width of the *data bus*.　　　3

   　(ii) State why computers do not come with the maximum addressable memory installed.　　　1

   　(iii) State the effect that adding **one** new line to the address bus would have on the maximum addressable memory.　　　1

   (c) Describe the function of each of the following in a memory *read* operation:

   　• 　address bus.

   　• 　data bus.

   　• 　control lines.　　　3

   (d) The laptop computer has several *utility programs* including a *disk defragmenter*.

   　(i) State what is meant by the term "utility program".　　　1

   　(ii) Fragmentation of the hard disk decreases the performance of the computer. Explain why performance decreases.　　　2

   (e) The laptop computer has anti-virus software. State an *anti-virus software detection technique*.　　　1

Marks

SECTION II (continued)

14. Murray Components is a small business that sells computer hardware. They have a shop that employs four people.

   (a) Networks can be set up as either *peer-to-peer* or *client server*.

   (i) In terms of data backup, describe **one** difference between a peer-to-peer network and a client server network. 2

   (ii) Murray Components have a peer-to-peer network with four workstations. Describe **one** reason why they may have chosen a peer-to-peer network. 2

   (b) Murray Components is advised that a *ring topology* is not the most suitable topology to use for their LAN.

   (i) Draw a **labelled** diagram of a ring topology. 2

   (ii) State a more suitable topology and state **one** advantage it has over a ring topology. 2

   (c) Murray Components requires a network printer to print advertising leaflets.

   (i) State **two** technical requirements that should be considered when selecting a suitable printer. 2

   (ii) State **two** roles of the *operating system* and describe how each is used to ensure that data is printed correctly. 4

   (d) State **one** function of a *print server*. 1

   (e) Murray Components starts to sell much more *solid state* storage. State **two** reasons why solid state storage is becoming more popular. 2

[Turn over

Marks

SECTION II (continued)

15. RightIT, a software company, is currently developing a cash machine program for a bank. The cash machine will offer five options to customers.

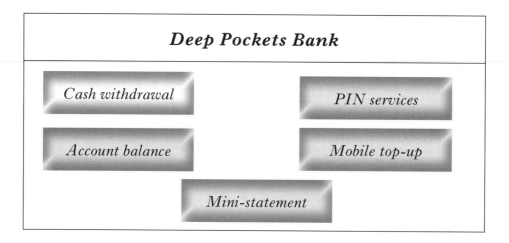

   (a) RightIT decided to use an *event-driven* programming language to write the software. State **two** reasons why an event-driven programming language is suitable for this software.   2

   (b)   (i) State **one** other type of programming language RightIT could have used for this software.   1

       (ii) Justify why it would also have been suitable.   1

   (c) The options selected during a day are stored as a list. The bank would like the software to calculate the number of times the **mobile top-up** option appears on this list. Use pseudocode to design an algorithm to carry out this calculation.   4

   (d) Once the software has been written RightIT carries out *systematic* testing. Explain how systematic testing is carried out.   2

   (e) The bank is anxious that RightIT also carries out *comprehensive* testing on the software. State what is meant by comprehensive testing.   1

   (f) The final version of the software is ready to be distributed to the bank. A *compiler* is chosen as the most suitable translator. Explain why a compiler is suitable at this stage.   2

   (g) Several months after the software has been in use, the bank asks RightIT to include another option in the menu. This option should allow customers to withdraw cash in Euros. Name the **type** of *maintenance* required and justify your answer.   2

Marks

SECTION II (continued)

16. Sidney is an experienced programmer. He decides to write a book called "The Good Programming Guide".

(*a*) Chapter one of the book is entitled "Characteristics of a well written program". Two characteristics of a well written program are *reliability* and *efficiency*.

　(i) Define the term "reliable".　**1**

　(ii) Explain **one** way in which a program can be written to make it efficient in terms of **processor** usage.　**2**

(*b*) A well written program should make use of *parameter passing*.

　(i) State the **purpose** of an *in parameter*.　**1**

　(ii) State the **purpose** of an *out parameter*.　**1**

(*c*) Chapter two of the book is entitled "Being a team player". Sidney is keen to emphasise that on most projects there will be a team of programmers writing the software. Describe **one** example of how a programming team can ensure they will work together effectively.　**2**

(*d*) Another chapter is entitled "Saving time whilst programming". A *module library* will save programmers time as they will not have to code or test these modules independently. State **one** further benefit of making use of a module library.　**1**

(*e*) When working with data, the use of *1-D arrays* can save time.

　(i) State **two** characteristics of a 1-D array.　**2**

　(ii) Data can be stored using individual variables or using a 1-D array. Describe how the use of a 1-D array can save time when writing a program compared to several individual variables.　**2**

(*f*) Sidney sets a short programming challenge at the end of each chapter. One of these programs involves identifying a computing term from another computing related word. For example, "ram" from "program".

Using code from a programming environment with which you are familiar, show how you would extract the term **"ram"** from **"program"**, when "program" has been assigned to the variable called "word".　**2**

(60)

word
program

　[END OF SECTION II]　**[Turn over**

Page seven

[BLANK PAGE]

SECTION III

Attempt one sub-section of Section III.

For the sub-section chosen, attempt *all* questions.

Marks

SECTION III

PART A — Artificial Intelligence

Attempt all questions.

17. An "intelligent" computer system has been designed to compete against people on a televised quiz show. A human presenter reads out a question and the contestant quickest to respond gets to answer the question.

Some examples of the quiz questions are shown below:

Question	Answer
What word means a water sport and also browsing the web?	Surfing
What word meaning "also" sounds like a number?	Too
Which animal is known as "the ship of the desert"?	Camel

(a) (i) The computer system requires the ability to process *natural language*. State **two** other aspects of intelligence involved in playing this quiz game. 2

(ii) Explain why **this** computer system better justifies a claim of "artificial intelligence" than a chess system developed to play the world champion at chess. 2

(b) The first stage of natural language processing is *speech recognition*.

(i) Name and describe the **two** other stages of *natural language processing* that the computer system will use. 4

(ii) Describe **one** difficulty in natural language processing using the quiz questions to illustrate your answer. 2

(c) Speed of response is important when playing the game. Describe how **one** advance in hardware would improve response times. 2

Marks

SECTION III

PART A — Artificial Intelligence (continued)

18. A Scottish law firm is involved in the development of an expert system that will be used on the World Wide Web. The purpose of the expert system is to create legal documents after an online consultation with a client.

    (*a*) (i) Name and describe **two** components of an *expert system shell*. 4

    (ii) The *expert system* will use *working memory* when consulting with a client. State **one** way in which information will be added to working memory during a consultation. 1

    (*b*) Once created, the expert system will be rigorously tested.

    (i) Explain the importance of testing during the software development process. 2

    (ii) State **two** reasons why it is important for the law firm to be involved in the testing of an expert system. 2

    (*c*) Explain why making this expert system available online might lead to difficulties for anyone using the system. 2

    (*d*) Describe **one** situation where a lawyer is better at providing legal documents than an expert system. 2

    (*e*) Name and describe another real world application of an expert system with which you are familiar. 2

[Turn over

Marks

SECTION III

PART A — Artificial Intelligence (continued)

19. The "six stones" puzzle starts with three black counters and three white counters on a board with seven spaces as shown:

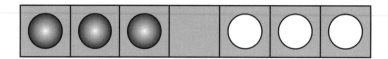

The puzzle is solved when the black and the white counters have swapped places. However, black counters can only move right and white counters can only move left according to the following four possible moves:

1. A black counter can move one space to the right into an empty space

2. A black counter can jump to the right over a white counter into an empty space

3. A white counter can move one space to the left into an empty space

4. A white counter can jump to the left over a black counter into an empty space.

(a) A search tree is shown below with the first move already completed.

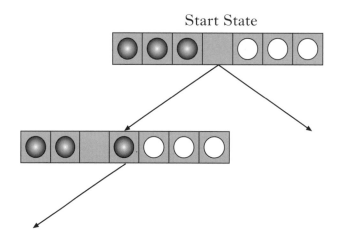

Start State

   (i) Draw the node that would be generated next if *breadth-first* searching is used.   1

   (ii) Draw the node that would be generated next if *depth-first* searching is used.   1

   (iii) Use the "six stones" puzzle to explain the term *backtracking* in depth-first searching.   2

(b) State **two** advantages of breadth-first when compared to depth-first searching.   2

(c) State another method of searching large search trees.   1

Marks

SECTION III

PART A — Artificial Intelligence (continued)

20. A company offers flights to various destinations stated below.

> There are direct flights from Glasgow to London and from London to Paris. Direct flights from Paris go to Rome and Seville. There is also a direct flight from Rome to Berlin.

(a) Represent the information in the paragraph above using a *semantic net*.　3

The company creates a knowledge base to provide information on their flights.

1. direct(glasgow london).　　　　　　　　　*There is a direct flight from Glasgow to London.*

2. direct(london paris).
3. direct(paris rome).
4. direct(paris seville).
5. direct (rome berlin).

6. fly_direct(P Q) IF direct(P Q).　　　　*You can fly directly from P to Q if there is direct flight from P to Q.*

7. one_stop(X Y) IF fly_direct(X Z) AND fly_direct(Z Y).　*There is only one stop in the flight from X to Y if you can fly directly from X to Z and fly directly from Z to Y.*

(b) Explain the term *sub-goal*.　2

(c) State the solutions to the query:

　　? direct(paris X)　2

(d) State the complex query that will determine which airport can fly to both Rome and Seville.　2

(e) Use the line numbers to trace the solution to the following query as far as the **first** solution.

　　? one_stop(glasgow Y)

In your answer you will be given credit for the correct use of the term *instantiation/instantiated*.　7

(50)

[*END OF SECTION III—PART A*]

Marks

SECTION III

PART B — Computer Networking

21. A holiday park has a website on the Internet.

Below is part of the home page for the holiday park.

(a) The *HTML* code required to create this part of the home page is shown below. Identify the **tags** represented by **A**, **B** and **C**.

<*A*>
  <head>
  <*B*>Bailey's Holiday Park</*B*>
  </head>
      <*C*>
      <h1>Welcome to the World of Family Fun</h1>
      </*C*>
</*A*>

3

(b) A software development company was appointed to create this website. State the **job title** of the person who should keep the project on track and within timescale and budget.

1

(c) The holiday park has many activities on offer such as cycling or rock climbing. There are a limited number of spaces available for each activity. The website allows guests to book and pay for these activities online before going on holiday.

(i) Describe **one** benefit to the customer of booking these activities online.

2

(ii) The holiday park notices that the number of activities booked has increased. State **one** possible reason for this increase.

1

(iii) Customers are worried about the security aspect of paying online for these activities. State **one** way that the holiday park could reassure customers that paying online is safe.

1

(d) The software development company has created some web pages using *WML* code so that they can be displayed in a *WAP* browser. WML code is more limited than HTML code. State **two** limitations of WML code when creating the web pages.

2

Marks

SECTION III

PART B — Computer Networking (continued)

22. A car sales company has many branches throughout the United Kingdom. Details of all cars for sale are accessible through their *intranet*.

(*a*) A salesperson has to download a 200 Megabyte file which is stored on the central file server. The actual file downloads at a speed of 512 kilobits per second. Calculate the time taken in minutes for this file to be downloaded using this connection. Express your answer to one decimal place.

2

(*b*) The *OSI* model is a set of protocols used within computer networks. State the **purpose** of the OSI model.

1

(*c*) Two protocols used to transmit data are HTTP and TCP/IP.

(i) Describe the role of the IP protocol when transmitting data over an intranet.

2

(ii) Name **one** other protocol that could be used to transfer files across an intranet.

1

(*d*) When sending data across a network, *packet switching* may be used. Describe how packet switching operates.

3

(*e*) A *parity check* is carried out when transmitting data around a network.

(i) Describe **one** situation where a parity check would fail to detect an error. Use an example to illustrate your answer.

2

(ii) Explain **one** way in which using a parity check decreases network performance.

1

[Turn over

Marks

SECTION III

PART B — Computer Networking (continued)

23. Ti-Ket Web is a small ticket agency. Ti-Ket Web sells event tickets over the telephone or on the Internet.

(a)   (i) *"A rival company sends millions of simultaneous online requests to generate a ticket availability report for a particular concert. At this point the system is inaccessible to normal user requests."*

    Name the type of server attack described above.   **1**

  (ii) State **two** financial consequences of this attack on Ti-Ket Web.   **2**

  (iii) Describe **two** ways in which the use of a firewall could help to prevent Ti-Ket Web from further attacks.   **2**

(b) Ti-Ket Web has a local area network. This network has a *switch*. Explain **one** reason why Ti-Ket Web decided to add a switch rather than a *hub* to the local area network.   **2**

(c) The IP addresses for some of the devices on the network are as follows:

Computer 1	198.169.120.100	File Server	198.169.120.103
Computer 2	198.169.120.101	Router	198.169.120.104
Computer 3	198.169.120.102	Printer	198.169.120.105

  (i) State the *class* of IP address used within this network. Justify your answer.   **2**

A new computer is added to the network. It is allocated the IP address **198.198.120.278**

  (ii) State **one** reason why the second octet is invalid.   **1**

  (iii) State **one** reason why the fourth octet is invalid.   **1**

(d) *Carrier Sense Multiple Access with Collision Detection* (CSMA/CD) is used on this network to control which node can transmit at any one time. State **two** ways in which CSMA/CD might increase transmission time.   **2**

Marks

SECTION III

PART B — Computer Networking (continued)

24. Many families use the Internet to search for information and communicate using e-mail.

(a) A *meta-search engine* can be used to find information on the World Wide Web.

    (i) Explain how a meta-search engine works.   **3**

    (ii) Name **one** method that a search engine could use to build its indexes.   **1**

(b) State the purpose of SMTP.   **1**

Social networking sites are used by many children to communicate with other people.

(c) State **two** reasons why some parents may be concerned about their children accessing such sites.   **2**

(d)   (i) A parent has set up a *walled garden*. Explain the term "walled garden".   **2**

    (ii) His child uses the Internet for homework. State why the child may **not** be happy with the walled garden.   **1**

    (iii) An alternative method that the parent could use is "Internet filtering software". Explain why this would be more suitable for the child.   **1**

(e) Some people believe that access to the Internet leads to an *Information Rich* society.

    (i) Explain the term "Information Rich".   **2**

    (ii) State **two** benefits of being Information Rich.   **2**

    (50)

[END OF SECTION III—PART B]

[Turn over

Marks

SECTION III

PART C — Multimedia Technology

25. The logo for a new business has been drawn on paper and then scanned into a computer. The logo is shown below.

(*a*) (i) *CCDs* are used by both scanners and digital cameras when capturing an image. Explain how the CCD in a scanner differs from those in a digital camera.

2

   (ii) The edges of the scanned logo appeared slightly jagged. *Anti-aliasing* was used to smooth the edges. Describe how anti-aliasing achieves this.

2

   (iii) Explain how *resampling* might remove the jagged edges.

2

(*b*) It is suggested that the logo may be stored as a vector graphic. Explain why this logo should be stored as a vector graphic rather than a bitmapped graphic.

2

Marks

SECTION III

PART C — Multimedia Technology (continued)

26. The members of the Metro Gnome Jazz Club have decided to create a club website. Members are allowed to download files; visitors can *stream* files.

(*a*) (i) Explain the term "stream".   1

    (ii) Describe **one** advantage to the Jazz Club of only allowing visitors to stream files.   2

Codecs play an important role during the streaming of files and can be implemented in hardware or software.

(*b*) A codec codes and decodes streamed files. State **two** other purposes of a codec during the streaming of a file.   2

(*c*) Explain the benefit of having codecs implemented in hardware when receiving streamed multimedia files.   2

The website includes a library of sound files stored in MIDI, WAV and MP3 formats.

(*d*) Two of the attributes stored in MIDI files are *duration* and *tempo*. Name **one** other attribute stored in a MIDI file.   1

(*e*) State **one** type of sound for which MIDI is unsuitable.   1

A particular piece of music is stored in MIDI and MP3 file formats. Both files are the same size.

(*f*) (i) Explain **one** advantage of storing files in MIDI rather than MP3 file format.   1

    (ii) A member downloads both versions of the file. Explain why the sound differs when each file is played back.   2

    (iii) State **two** ways that compression is achieved in the MP3 file format.   2

[Turn over

Marks

SECTION III

PART C — Multimedia Technology (continued)

27. David is a car racing fan. He records short video clips of races at a local circuit and transfers the clips to his computer for editing. David uses video editing software to join the video clips taken into one continuous video clip.

    (*a*) When he joins the clips together, David uses the *timeline* and *transition* features.

        (i) Explain why the timeline feature will be useful for David when he is producing the single continuous clip.   1

        (ii) Name **one** transition David could use.   1

    (*b*) One of David's video clips plays for 4 minutes. David recorded the clip using 24 bit colour with a resolution of 720,000 pixels per frame at 15 frames per second. Calculate the file size of the uncompressed video. Show all working and express your answer in appropriate units.   3

    (*c*) David stores some video clips in the MPEG file format. Describe how MPEG achieves compression.   3

    (*d*) David stores other video clips in the AVI file format. Unlike MPEG, AVI does not allow compression. State **two** reasons why the AVI format might still be a suitable file format for some video clips.   2

    (*e*) David has old analogue video recordings that he is transferring onto his computer. Describe the roles of the ADC and DSP on the video capture card during the transfer.   2

Marks

SECTION III

PART C — Multimedia Technology (continued)

28. Super Tutorials create multimedia lessons.

(*a*) All the lessons begin with the Super Tutorials theme tune. The tune plays for 1 minute and was recorded in 32 bit stereo using a sampling frequency of 44.1 kilohertz. Ignoring compression, calculate the file size for the theme tune. Express your answer in appropriate units and show all working. **3**

The multimedia lessons include text, video and a voice track.

(*b*) Lesson voice tracks are initially stored using the RAW file format. State the name of the **technique** used to convert the analogue signal into a digital form. **1**

(*c*) The completed lessons, which include video and voiceover sound files, are usually distributed in the RIFF file format.

    (i) The RIFF file format is an example of a *container file*. Explain the term "container file". **2**

    (ii) Explain the benefit of using container files in the distribution of multimedia files. **2**

(*d*) During testing some problems were found with the voice tracks. It was noted that some voice tracks were too loud but others were too quiet.

    (i) Name and describe the function of sound editing software which could be used to make the voice tracks play at the same volume. **2**

One voice track file also contained some unclear words. The waveform for part of this file shows the problem.

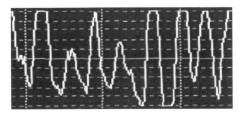

    (ii) State the term for this problem. **1**

    (iii) The problem identified in Question (*d*)(ii) may have been caused by recording at too high a volume setting. State **one** other possible reason for this problem. **1**

[Turn over for Question 28 (continued) on *Page twenty-two*

Marks

SECTION III

PART C — Multimedia Technology (continued)

28. (continued)

(e) Super Tutorials also supplies lessons on DVD. It has been suggested to Super Tutorials that *holographic* disks may replace DVDs in the future.

  (i) Describe how the physical storage of data on a holographic disk differs from a DVD. **2**

  (ii) Holographic disks allow faster data transfer than DVDs. Explain **why** this is the case. **2**

(50)

[END OF SECTION III—PART C]

[END OF QUESTION PAPER]

HIGHER

2012

[BLANK PAGE]

X206/12/01

NATIONAL QUALIFICATIONS 2012	THURSDAY, 31 MAY 9.00 AM – 11.30 AM	COMPUTING HIGHER

Attempt **all** questions in Section I.

Attempt **all** questions in Section II.

Attempt **one** sub-section of Section III.

Part A	Artificial Intelligence	Page 12	Questions 23 to 27
Part B	Computer Networking	Page 18	Questions 28 to 31
Part C	Multimedia Technology	Page 22	Questions 32 to 35

For the sub-section chosen, attempt **all** questions.

Read all questions carefully.

Do not write on the question paper.

Write as neatly as possible.

SECTION I

Marks

Attempt all questions in this section.

1. Write the ten digit binary number **1001001001** as a positive integer.

   1

2. A computer system uses *floating point representation* to store *real* numbers.

   (a) State the part of floating point representation that determines the **range** of numbers stored.

   1

   (b) State the part of floating point representation that determines the **precision** of numbers stored.

   1

3. Ali has created a poster using *bitmapped* graphic software. Describe how a bitmapped graphic is stored.

   2

4. *Protocol conversion* and *buffering* are two functions of an interface. State **two** other functions of an interface.

   2

5. The table shows types of computer memory listed in **descending** order of *speed of access*, (fastest first). Identify the **two** missing types (1) and (3).

(1)	
(2)	Cache
(3)	
(4)	Backing store

   2

6. Audrey creates and saves a new document to the hard disk.

   (a) State **two** tasks carried out by the *file management* part of the operating system during this save operation.

   2

   (b) State **one** task carried out by the *input/output management* part of the operating system during this save operation.

   1

SECTION I (continued)   *Marks*

7. The diagram below shows the layout of a small LAN.

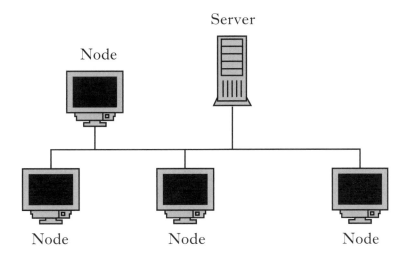

Server

Node

Node   Node   Node

(a) Name this network *topology*.   1

(b) The network shown above is a *client server* network. State **one** advantage of a
client server network over a *peer-to-peer* network.   1

(c) A device is required to connect this network to the Internet. Name this device.   1

8. The software development process is *iterative*. Explain how the word iterative
applies to this process.   2

9. Many software development projects use *top-down design*. Explain the process of
top-down design.   1

10. Name **one** *graphical design notation*.   1

11. An *interpreter* may be used in the software development process.

(a) Name **one** stage of the software development process where the interpreter
may be used.   1

(b) Explain how the interpreter is used in the stage named in part (a).   1

12. Describe **one** difference between a *scripting* language and a *procedural* language.   2

Marks

SECTION I (continued)

13. (*a*) State what is meant by a *boolean* variable.   1

    (*b*) Explain how a boolean variable could be used in a *linear search* algorithm.   1

14. Software should be both *reliable* and *robust*. Explain the terms "reliable" and "robust".   2

15. State **one** way in which documentation produced at the *testing* stage of the software development process will be used during *corrective* maintenance.   1

16. State **two** characteristics of programming code that improve *maintainability*.   2

    (30)

SECTION II   *Marks*

Attempt all questions in this section.

17. Tara, who works for Consumer Friend Magazine, has produced the following table.

Consumer Friend Magazine				
Processor	Clock Speed (GHz)	MIPS	MegaFLOPs	Data Bus Width (Bits)
Inrel Core Gi	3·2	72,495	63,933	64
Atheton E	2·8	73,665	63,105	64
Motorilla T	2·0	49,924	51,150	128

NOTE: One MegaFLOP = One Million FLOPs

(a) Explain why clock speed alone is not considered a good measure of **processor** performance.   1

(b) Tara states that the Atheton E is better than the Inrel Core Gi as it has a higher MIPS result. Explain why Tara may be incorrect.   2

(c) A computer containing the Motorilla T has a 32 bit address bus, a 128 bit data bus and 24 control lines. Calculate the maximum addressable memory of this computer.

Show all working. State your answer using appropriate units.   3

(d) All processors contain an *ALU* and a *control unit*.

   (i) State **one** logic operation performed by the ALU.   1

   (ii) Describe the purpose of the control unit.   1

(e) The manufacturers of the Inrel Core Gi are considering using a wider data bus in a new processor design. State **one** reason why this will improve processor performance.   1

[Turn over

SECTION II (continued)

Marks

18. A system called EarthWatch gathers data from weather stations all over the world. Each station uses a *terminal* to enter data into the EarthWatch *mainframe*.

    (a) Apart from the physical size or the cost of a mainframe, explain **one** difference between a mainframe with terminals and a network of computers.

    2

    (b) The mainframe's hard disk system has been continually storing weather data for 5 years. A message appeared on the main screen stating that the data file could not be stored on the hard disk due to lack of storage space. However there is enough space on the mainframe's hard disk system.

        (i) Explain the **most likely** cause of this apparent lack of storage.

        2

        (ii) Name a piece of software which could solve the problem identified in (i).

        1

        (iii) State the **class** of software that the item named in (ii) belongs to.

        1

    (c) Each EarthWatch weather station contains 10 terminals connected to a file server situated 80 metres from the terminals. State a suitable transmission medium to connect the terminals to the server. Explain your reasoning.

    2

    (d) The EarthWatch mainframe performs many memory read operations per second. Write down the steps involved in a single memory read operation. Name the *bus* or *control lines* involved at each step.

    3

SECTION II (continued)   *Marks*

19. Harry is an expert on human linguistics. He is currently studying a **data file** on his computer containing 3000 ancient Chinese characters.

    (*a*) State whether this file is an *ASCII* file or a *UNICODE* file. Explain your reasoning.   **2**

    (*b*) Harry buys a printer to print the characters. Apart from cost, name **two** other relevant characteristics of a printer.   **2**

    (*c*) Harry is concerned that this data file may contain a *file virus*.

        (i) Explain whether Harry's concern is justified.   **2**

        (ii) State what is meant by a computer virus.   **1**

        (iii) State **one** action of a virus.   **1**

    (*d*) Harry saves a picture of each character in GIF format. State **two** characteristics of the GIF format.   **2**

[Turn over

SECTION II (continued)

Marks

20. Martin is a systems analyst. He has just been given a new project to work on.

    (a) (i) Explain why Martin will interview the client during the *analysis* stage.   **1**

        (ii) State **two** other techniques that Martin may use during the analysis stage.   **2**

    (b) Martin is responsible for producing a document at the **end** of the analysis stage.

        (i) Name this document.   **1**

        (ii) State **two** reasons why this document has to be agreed with the client before it is finalised.   **2**

    (c) Explain how a systems analyst could be involved in the **testing** stage of a project.   **1**

    (d) When Martin was at University, he earned money by being part of *independent test groups*. Explain why he cannot be part of the independent test group assigned to **this** project.   **1**

    (e) Effective testing of the software needs to be both *systematic* and *comprehensive*. Explain the terms "systematic" and "comprehensive".   **2**

    (f) Towards the end of the project, Martin is told that the project is running over budget. State the **job title** of the person who has the responsibility for the project budget.   **1**

SECTION II (continued)   *Marks*

21. Over the summer, a garden centre has been running a "tallest sunflower" competition.

Entrants have completed an online entry form to provide their name and the height of their sunflower. These have been collated into two lists. Samples from these lists are shown below.

Name of entrant	Height of sunflower (metres)
Eildih Brown	2·15
Helen Atkins	1·79
Mark Ames	2·32
Jenna Wylie	1·41

(a) State the *data structure* and *data type* used to store the list of heights.   2

(b) Using *pseudocode*, design an algorithm to find and display the **name** of the person growing the tallest sunflower.   6

(c) The garden centre wants to give a consolation prize to the grower of the **shortest** sunflower. A number of changes need to be made to the pseudocode you wrote in part (b).

  (i) State **one** change that you would make to your pseudocode from part (b).   1

  (ii) Explain **why** this change is necessary.   1

[Turn over

SECTION II (continued)

Marks

22. A travel agent uses a suite of software to help advertise holidays and make bookings. Part of the pseudocode that was written for the software is:

---

if cost per person is less than 500
    set band to 'cheap'
end if

if cost per person is greater than or equal to 500 AND cost per person is less than 2000
    set band to 'medium'
end if

if cost per person is greater than or equal to 2000
    set band to 'expensive'
end if

(a) By using a holiday cost per person of £495, explain why this pseudocode would not produce *efficient* code. **2**

(b) Show how these lines could be rewritten in a more efficient way. **2**

(c) When the above is implemented as a subroutine, state whether the variable "cost per person" would be passed by *reference* or *value*. Justify your answer. **2**

Each holiday booking is assigned a unique reference code. The software which creates this code uses *concatenation* within a *user-defined function*.

(d) Explain the term *concatenation*. **1**

(e) Explain the term *function*. **2**

(60)

[END OF SECTION II]

SECTION III

Attempt one sub-section of Section III.

For the sub-section chosen, attempt *all* questions.

SECTION III

Marks

PART A — Artificial Intelligence

Attempt all questions.

23. The Turing Test can be used during the development of *chatterbots*.

    (a) State the purpose of the Turing Test.   **1**

    (b) Describe how a chatterbot attempts to have a meaningful conversation.   **2**

    (c) State **two** weaknesses that may be present in a chatterbot's conversation with a human.   **2**

    (d) State **one** improvement in processors and describe how it improves the performance of a chatterbot.   **2**

24. The water jugs puzzle is a well known artificial intelligence problem. In this puzzle there are two jugs; the jug on the left holds three litres and the one on the right holds five litres. Neither has any measuring markers on it. There is a tap that can be used to fill the jugs with water. The goal of the puzzle is to measure exactly four litres of water.

5 litre

3 litre

A computer is used to find a solution.

    (a) State the aspect of intelligence which a computer is demonstrating when finding the solution to the water jugs puzzle.   **1**

    (b) Some people would argue that a computer solving this puzzle does **not** have artificial intelligence.

    State **one** reason which supports this opinion.   **1**

SECTION III   *Marks*

PART A — Artificial Intelligence (continued)

24. (continued)

The computer represents both jugs being empty as (0,0). The node (3,0) means that the three litre jug on the left is full and that the five litre jug on the right is empty.

It attempts to solve the puzzle by generating the following states:

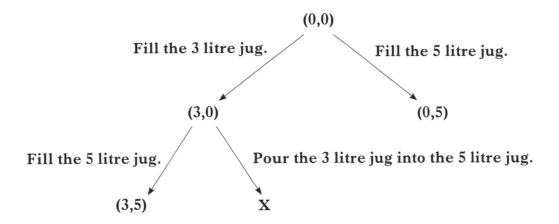

(c) Name this type of diagram.   1

(d) The order of nodes currently in memory is (0,0), (3,0), (0,5) and (3,5).

   Explain which *search technique* is being used.   2

(e) State **two** other search techniques that could be used.   2

(f) State the node missing from the diagram, marked by the letter X.   1

(g) The diagram shows three of the possible moves:

   • Fill the 3 litre jug
   • Fill the 5 litre jug
   • Pour the 3 litre jug into the 5 litre jug

   State **two** other possible moves.   2

[Turn over

SECTION III

Marks

PART A — Artificial Intelligence (continued)

25. CeramicSee is a vision system that is used in the quality control of ceramic tiles.

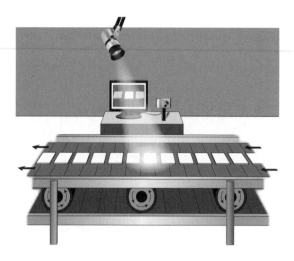

CeramicSee rejects tiles with flaws such as:

- wrong shade or colour

- physical damage such as chips or scratches.

(a) Describe **two** ways in which CeramicSee overcomes common problems with vision systems.　　2

(b) The *image acquisition* stage of CeramicSee uses a digital camera capable of 32 bit colour to capture an image of a tile. Calculate the maximum number of different colours in an image.　　1

(c) Name and describe **two** other stages of computer vision.　　4

(d) CeramicSee uses an *artificial neural system* to identify defective tiles. Describe how *weights* are used in the **training** of an artificial neural system.　　3

(e) State **another** example of an application that uses an *embedded* vision system.　　1

SECTION III

Marks

PART A — Artificial Intelligence (continued)

26. Intelligent robots are one application of artificial intelligence. This has resulted in the development of robots for household tasks particularly floor cleaning.

Floor cleaning robot

(*a*) State what is meant by the term "artificial intelligence".

1

(*b*) State **one** characteristic of an intelligent robot when compared to a dumb robot.

1

(*c*) Describe **two practical** difficulties associated with the development and use of an intelligent robot for floor cleaning.

2

(*d*)   (i) State **one** legal implication of the use of an intelligent robot.

1

    (ii) Explain how a manufacturer of robots can address legal implications.

1

[Turn over

SECTION III

Marks

PART A — Artificial Intelligence (continued)

27. An online multi-player game has been created. Each player in the game is a character such as a troll or an orc that can acquire various objects as they move through the game eg a sword or armour. A character can only defeat another if they have the correct object.

    This knowledge base stores the current state of the game:

1.	has_found(troll jewel).	*The troll has found a jewel.*
2.	has_found(troll sword).	
3.	has_found(orc armour).	
4.	has_found(druid potion).	
5.	has_found(druid lance).	
6.	is_weapon_against(lance troll).	*The lance is the weapon to use against a troll.*
7.	is_weapon_against(sword orc).	
8.	is_weapon_against(jewel troll).	
9.	life_points(troll 1000).	*The troll has 1000 life points.*
10.	life_points(orc 200).	
11.	life_points(druid 140).	

    12. stronger_than(X Y) IF life_points(X A) AND life_points(Y B) AND A>B.

    Character X is stronger than character Y if X has life point A and character Y has life points B and A is greater than B.

    13. can_defeat(X Y) IF has_found(X Z) AND is_weapon_against(Z Y) AND not(X=Y).

    Character X can defeat character Y if character X has found item Z and Z is the weapon against character Y and character X is not character Y.

    (a) State the solution to the following query:

    ? has_found(X potion)

    1

    (b) State the query required to find the weapons that can be used against the troll.

    2

SECTION III

PART A — Artificial Intelligence (continued)

27. (continued)

(c) Explain how the following query would be evaluated:

? not(life_points(troll 800))

2

(d) Trace the **first** solution to the query:

? can_defeat(troll Y)

In your answer you will be given credit for the correct use of *backtrack*.

8

(e) The original software specification stated that a player can defeat an opponent if the player has found the appropriate weapon for that opponent and that they are stronger than the opponent.

   (i) The existing rule 13 must have **one** line added to meet this requirement.

```
can_defeat(X Y) IF has_found(X Z) AND
                    is_weapon_against(Z Y) AND
                    not(X = Y) AND
                    ........................................
```

   State the missing line of the new rule.

2

   (ii) State the **type** of maintenance that this change to the software is best described as.

1

(50)

[END OF SECTION III—PART A]

[Turn over

SECTION III

Marks

PART B — Computer Networking

Attempt all questions.

28. It is important that computer networks are designed to agreed standards, such as the Open Systems Interconnection (OSI).

    (*a*) (i) State the name of the *layer* of the OSI model at which a *router* functions.   1

           (ii) State the name of the *layer* of the OSI model that carries out *data encryption*.   1

    (*b*) *TCP/IP* is a set of protocols used in network communication. State the actions carried out by the **IP** part when transmitting data over a network.   2

    (*c*) Explain how *CSMA/CD* improves network performance.   2

    (*d*) The byte of data below is transmitted across a network. It contains a *parity* bit.

    1000 1111

    State which **kind** of parity was used when sending this data. Justify your answer.   2

    (*e*) Data can be sent *synchronously* or *asynchronously*. State which of these methods uses start and stop bits and how it uses them.   2

SECTION III

Marks

PART B — Computer Networking (continued)

29. A local dentist has created a cabled network to connect his four computers and a printer.

    (a) Explain why the dentist chose to use cables rather than wireless to connect the network.   **1**

    (b) The dentist is worried that a hacker may get access to his patient files without his knowledge. Name the **type** of attack that the dentist is worried about.   **1**

    A website is being created for the dentist using *HTML* as shown below.

    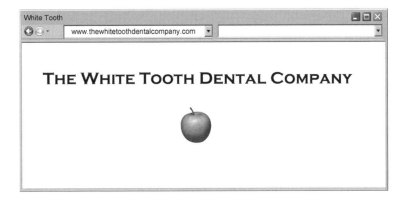

    (c) Write the HTML code for the **title tag** of this webpage.   **2**

    (d) The apple image displayed on the web page was captured in *true colour*. State what is meant by "true colour".   **1**

    (e) The website is published on the Internet. However, the dentist realises that search engines are not finding his website.

        (i) State an additional element that should be included in the HTML code in order to help a search engine find the website.   **1**

        (ii) Name the section of the HTML code in which this element should be placed.   **1**

    (f) The dentist would like the website to be viewed on mobile phones. The *HTML* code will have to be re-written in a different language.

        (i) Name the language required to create webpages for mobile phones.   **1**

        (ii) State the protocol that allows mobile phones to access the website.   **1**

        (iii) State **one** other type of device that uses this protocol.   **1**

    (g) After testing the mobile phone version of the website, an error was found. State the type of *maintenance* required to fix errors not identified during testing.   **1**

SECTION III

Marks

PART B — Computer Networking (continued)

30. A teacher requires a username and password to give her remote access to her school server.

(a) Other than *TCP/IP*, name a protocol which could allow remote access to a server.

1

(b) The school's server has been subjected to a *denial of service (DOS) attack*.

   (i) Describe **one** possible denial of service attack.

2

   (ii) State **two financial** implications for the school as a result of this DOS attack.

2

(c) The school's server has a *firewall*. State **two** ways that a firewall could be used to monitor access to the school network.

2

(d) Hacking is a **security** issue that the school will have to consider. Other than a firewall, describe **two** software methods that the school could employ to try to prevent hackers from gaining unauthorised access to their server.

4

(e) The school is concerned about accidental or malicious loss of data from their server. They have installed a *mirror disk*. Explain how a mirror disk would help them in this situation.

2

(f) The school is concerned about staff and pupils accessing websites from school computers.

   (i) Explain how a *walled garden* would prevent staff and pupils from accessing unsuitable websites.

2

   (ii) Describe **one** way that *Internet filtering* software differs from a walled garden.

1

(g) The teacher creates a *WPAN* to connect her laptop, printer and smartphone. Explain **one** reason why a *WPAN* would be appropriate for this network.

1

SECTION III

Marks

PART B — Computer Networking (continued)

31. A sports centre has a local area network of 10 computers and 2 printers.

(a) Explain why *class A IP addressing* is **not** suitable for this network.

1

(b) A network interface card is required to provide a physical link to the local area network. The network interface card contains a *MAC* address. Describe the purpose of a MAC address.

1

(c) When data is transmitted across the network a *Cyclic Redundancy Check* (CRC) is carried out. Describe how the **receiving** device uses CRC.

3

(d) The sports centre has a website which allows bookings to be made and paid for online. Members have expressed some security concerns about using their credit cards to pay for bookings online.

(i) Explain how *packet switching* would increase the security of the transmitted data.

2

(ii) The sports centre's network can also set up a direct communications link to their head office. State the method of switching which would set up this direct link.

1

(e) The sports centre has an *ADSL* connection to the Internet.

(i) The manager wants to download a 150 Megabyte file. The ADSL connection has a download speed of 8 Megabits per second. Calculate the time taken to download this file. Show all working.

2

(ii) When the file was downloaded it took longer than the time calculated in part (i). Suggest **two** reasons for this increase in download time.

2

(50)

[END OF SECTION III—PART B]

[Turn over

SECTION III

Marks

PART C — Multimedia Technology

Attempt all questions.

32. Peter is a guitar teacher who uses his website to give pupils access to audio files. The audio files are instrumental tracks for practice between lessons.

   (a) (i) The audio files are stored in the *MIDI* format. One benefit of this file format is its small size. State **two** other benefits of using the MIDI file format.   2

   (ii) MIDI files are stored using *sound attributes* such as *duration* and *tempo*. Describe the terms "duration" and "tempo".   2

   (b) State **two** reasons why the pupils may prefer the *MP3* file format to the MIDI file format.   2

   Peter has demonstration video clips on his website.

   (c) The video clips were originally taken using a resolution of 1024 × 768 with a frame rate of 25 fps. Calculate the file size of an uncompressed 24 bit video clip which plays for 64 seconds. Show all working. State your answer in megabytes.   3

   Pupils must *stream* the video clips to their computer when viewing.

   (d) Peter is worried about breach of copyright. Explain how **streaming** will help avoid this.   1

   (e) Assuming there are no hardware or software problems, explain why streamed video may pause when viewed on a pupil's computer.   2

SECTION III

Marks

PART C — Multimedia Technology (continued)

33. EasyVid manufactures video cameras. The EasyVid Super4 digital video camera will be a new digital video camera designed to replace the current EasyVid Power3 digital camera.

EasyVid Power3

4·1 megapixels
Bluetooth & Firewire enabled
40 Gb hard disk
Video editing software supplied

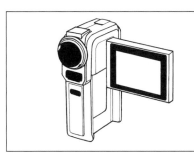

EasyVid Super4

12 megapixels
Bluetooth & USB 3·0 enabled
Built-in hardware codecs
Built-in 3 in 1 card reader
Video editing software supplied

(a) State **two** advantages USB 3·0 has over Firewire.   2

(b) It had been suggested that the EasyVid Super4 should be WiFi enabled. The manufacturer decides **not** to add a WiFi interface. State **one** reason other than cost to support their decision.   1

(c) The EasyVid Super4 has no hard disk. Explain why using removable solid state storage would extend battery life.   2

(d) The manufacturer has built in hardware *codecs* to the EasyVid Super4. Describe **one** advantage and **one** disadvantage to the user of a hardware codec rather than a software codec.   2

(e) Video editing software is provided with both cameras. This includes *transition features*.

   (i) Explain what is meant by a "transition feature".   1

   (ii) Name and describe **one** effect usually available as a transition.   2

(f) Explain why neither camera uses an *ADC* during data transfer to a computer.   1

[Turn over

SECTION III

Marks

PART C — Multimedia Technology (continued)

34. The Bestview Camera Club has an annual photographic competition. Presentation software is used to display the entries as a slide show.

(a) A design technique suitable for planning the presentation is storyboarding. Describe **two** features of a storyboard that should be included in the design of the presentation.

2

Spoken comments about entries are to be recorded for inclusion in the slide show.

(b) Calculate the **uncompressed** file size of an 8 bit, 24 second stereo recording sampled at 11 kHz. Show all working. State your answer in appropriate units.

3

The WAV file format is used to store the spoken comments. WAV files are compressed.

(c)   (i) State the name of the compression method used.

1

     (ii) Describe **how** this method achieves compression.

2

(d) Describe how the file size of a spoken comment could be significantly reduced without changing the sampling depth.

1

A short musical introduction is used at the start of the slide show. Figure 1 shows the waveform of the introduction. Figure 2 shows the waveform after an effect has been applied.

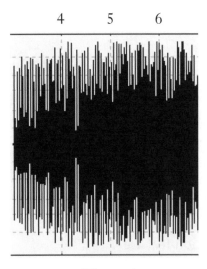

Figure 1

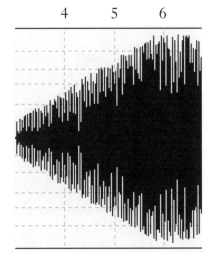

Figure 2

(e) State the effect applied to the sound.

1

SECTION III

Marks

PART C — Multimedia Technology (continued)

34. (continued)

(*f*) During testing of the slide show, it is noted that one audio file has been *clipped*.

   (i) Explain the term "clipping". You **must** include a diagram in your explanation.

2

   (ii) Describe how *normalisation* would have avoided the problem of clipping.

2

   (iii) Describe **one** disadvantage of normalisation.

2

[Turn over for Question 35 on *Page twenty-six*

SECTION III

Marks

PART C — Multimedia Technology (continued)

35. A designer has stored a graphic in each of *GIF*, *PNG* and *SVG* formats.

   (*a*) The designer notices that adding each circle to the graphic increases the file size of the SVG file but **not** the GIF or PNG files. Explain why the SVG file size increases.

           2

   (*b*) The finished graphic will be displayed on a variety of screen sizes. Explain why SVG might be the **best** format to choose in this situation.

           2

   (*c*) Part of the code for the smallest circle is changed from **rgb(0,78,0)** to **rgb(0,16,0)**. Describe the effect of this change on the circle.

           2

   (*d*) Dithering can be used with the GIF file format but is unnecessary with PNG.

     (i) Explain the term *dithering*.

           1

     (ii) Explain why dithering is not required for the PNG file format.

           2

   (*e*) The graphics software used by the designer includes *anti-aliasing*.

     (i) State the purpose of anti-aliasing.

           1

     (ii) Describe a situation when anti-aliasing might have to be used.

           1

           (50)

[END OF SECTION III—PART C]

[END OF QUESTION PAPER]

HIGHER

2013

[BLANK PAGE]

X206/12/01

NATIONAL QUALIFICATIONS 2013	TUESDAY, 28 MAY 9.00 AM – 11.30 AM	COMPUTING HIGHER

Attempt **all** questions in Section I.

Attempt **all** questions in Section II.

Attempt **one** sub-section of Section III.

Part A	Artificial Intelligence	Page 12	Questions 23 to 28
Part B	Computer Networking	Page 18	Questions 29 to 31
Part C	Multimedia Technology	Page 24	Questions 32 to 35

For the sub-section chosen, attempt **all** questions.

Read all questions carefully.

Do not write on the question paper.

Write as neatly as possible.

SECTION I

Marks

Attempt all questions in this section.

1. Characters can be stored using either *Unicode* or *ASCII*. State **one** advantage and **one** disadvantage of using Unicode when compared to ASCII.

    2

2. State the **minimum** number of bits needed to represent the range of positive whole numbers from 0 to 16777215.

    1

3. The image shown was created using a *bitmapped* graphics package.

    Describe how **bitmapped** graphics are stored.

    2

4. One possible threat to computers comes from *viruses*.

    (a) Name the **type** of computer virus that attaches itself to documents created in applications.

    1

    (b) Anti-virus software is often installed when a computer is set up. Describe **one** reason why the computer may still become infected.

    1

5. A school office has a networked laser printer.

    Name and describe a method that could be used to deal with **additional** print jobs when the printer's buffer is full.

    2

6. *Read* and *write* are two control lines. Name **two** other control lines.

    2

SECTION I (continued) *Marks*

7. Two *network topologies* are shown below. Describe the effect **on the network** of the failure of:

   • node X in Diagram A

   • node Y in Diagram B.

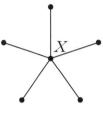

Key

• Node

⟍ Channel

Diagram A   Diagram B   2

8. The steps involved in a *write* to memory operation are given below. State the **two** missing steps.

   1 ....

   2 Data bus is set up with the data to be written.

   3 ....

   4 Data from data bus is placed into specified memory location.   2

9. State why *data flow* should be included in an algorithm.   1

10. The variable **firstTerm** contains "super" and the variable **secondTerm** contains "symmetry". The variable **physicsTerm** is assigned the value "supersymmetry". All three are *string* variables.

firstTerm	**secondTerm**	**physicsTerm**
super	symmetry	supersymmetry

   Using a programming language of your choice, show how *concatenation* is used to assign the value "supersymmetry" to the variable **physicsTerm**.   2

11. In the case of **both** a *local* variable and a *global* variable, explain what is meant by the term *scope*.   2

[Turn over

Marks

SECTION I (continued)

12. Describe **two** characteristics of a *1-D array*.

2

13. State **two** benefits of a *scripting* language.

2

14. State **one** reason why an *independent test group* may be used to test software.

1

15. Describe what is meant when a computer program is described as *portable*.

2

16. The documentation for each subroutine in a *module library* will identify the name of the subroutine. State one **other** item of information that might be included in such documentation.

1

17. The main screen from software containing information about the universe is shown.

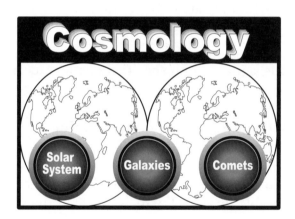

The **original specification** for the software required three buttons on the main screen. The client now requires a fourth button called Stars. State the **type** of *maintenance* required. Justify your answer.

2

(30)

[END OF SECTION I]

SECTION II

Marks

Attempt all questions in this section.

18. Formula One cars make use of computing technology during races. Every Formula One car is equipped with an on-board computer which records information during a race.

    (a) The on-board computer makes use of *solid state storage*. Other than robustness and cost, state **two** reasons why solid state storage is used.   2

    (b) During a race, measurements are made from temperature sensors. These sensors are connected to the on-board computer using interfaces. Name **two** functions of an interface that will be needed to transfer these measurements to the on-board computer and describe the operation of each during the transfer.   4

    Wiktoria regularly visits races to take photographs of the cars. She transfers them from her camera to her computer, edits them and uploads them to her website.

    (c) Wiktoria has bought a 12 Gigabyte flash card. She takes 4 inch by 6 inch photographs with a resolution of 1024 dpi and using 24-bit colour depth. Calculate the maximum number of photographs which can be stored on this card.

    Show all working.   4

    (d) Wiktoria transfers all of her pictures from the flash card to her hard disk. Name **two** functions of an operating system and describe how each will be involved in this process.   4

    (e) The writer of a new Formula One book discovers Wiktoria's website. He copies the pictures and puts them into his new book, which he then sells. Name the law which this writer has broken.   1

[Turn over

SECTION II (continued)

Marks

19. Colin recently started to work at a university. He was given funds to select a suite of computers for his lab. The IT department gave him two options to choose from.

	MegaPCII	PeartronIII
Clock Speed	3·4 GHz	3·6 GHz
Installed RAM	4 Gigabytes	8 Gigabytes
Maximum addressable RAM	32 Gigabytes	32 Gigabytes
Hard Disk	2 Terabytes	2 Terabytes
Cache Memory	8 Megabytes	8 Megabytes
Data bus	8 bit	64 bit

(a) Looking at the **MegaPCII**, Colin spots an obvious typing mistake in the information given. Identify the mistake and explain why it is incorrect. 2

(b) Calculate the width of the **address** bus for the **PeartronIII.** 3

(c) Both systems have *cache memory*. Explain how cache memory improves system performance. 2

(d) In order to make his choice, Colin uses the results of *application based tests*. State **two** reasons why Colin chose to use application based tests. 2

Computer systems in the university are networked in a *client/server network*.

(e) Explain one reason why a **peer-to-peer** network may not be suitable for the university. 2

(f) *Hubs* and *switches* are used in the university network. Explain **one** difference between a hub and a switch. 2

(g) All university computers have *anti-virus* software installed. Anti-virus is classed as *utility software*. State **two** other utility programs which are likely to be installed. 2

SECTION II (continued)

Marks

20. DeskCom create mathematics software for schools. A systems analyst from DeskCom has been sent to visit an interested school.

    (a) Describe **two** methods the systems analyst may use to gain knowledge of the school's current system for teaching mathematics.

    2

    (b) After the school visit, the systems analyst produces the *software specification* for creating new mathematics software for the school. State **two** purposes of this document.

    2

    (c) The initial design for the new mathematics software was created using a *graphical design notation*. Name **one** graphical design notation.

    1

    (d) *Top down design* and *stepwise refinement* will also be used in the design of the mathematics software. Explain the terms "top down design" and "stepwise refinement".

    2

    (e) DeskCom programmers will consider many factors when deciding which programming language to use to code the new software. Describe **one** factor they should consider when choosing a programming language.

    1

    (f) It is important that the new mathematics software is *efficient*. Describe **two** items of **evidence** that could be gathered to support measurement of the efficiency of code.

    2

[Turn over

SECTION II (continued)

Marks

21. ModernCorp manufacture tablet computers. Their recent sales initiative is shown.

Tablet Computer Price	Discount Rate %
<=£500	10
>£500 and <£1000	12
>=£1000	15

A program is to be created to calculate the **discount rate** due.

(a) The price of a tablet computer is held in the variable **price**. The discount to be applied is stored in the variable **discountRate**. Use **pseudocode** to design an algorithm, which uses a *CASE* statement (or equivalent) to assign the correct discount rate.

3

MoodyZak is software which comes free with a ModernCorp tablet computer. MoodyZak creates a song list from stored music based on data entered about the user's mood. Mood data is entered into MoodyZak, through a touch screen, on a list of check boxes.

Dark   Sad   Bored   Quiet   Bright   Happy

(b) State a *data structure* and *data type* that could be used to record the mood list for a single song.

2

(c) The use of a *declarative* programming language was considered for the creation of MoodyZak. Explain why a declarative programming language might be suitable in this case.

2

(d) The use of check boxes as the input for MoodyZak is an *event driven* feature. State the meaning of the term "event driven".

1

(e) The author of the MoodyZak code did not provide any supporting documentation. Only the compiled program, the program listing and a software licence were provided. Describe **two** examples of problems that this missing documentation could cause.

2

SECTION II (continued)

Marks

22. A horse race produced the set of results shown below. The names and times are held as two lists.

Name	Mister McGee	Kelly's Hero	Fred's Folly	The Tool Inns	Fizzy Lizzie
Time: *Minutes*	8·15	7·12	8·65	9·15	7·08

   (*a*)   (i) Use **pseudocode** to design an algorithm that would store the **time** of the **winning** horse in the variable **Fastest**.　4

          (ii) The time for the **Slowest** horse is also to be identified. Other than the change of variable name, state **one** change that would have to be made to your algorithm for part (i) to achieve this.　1

        (iii) The number of horses who have a race time greater than 8 minutes is also to be identified. State the name of a *standard algorithm* that could achieve this.　1

   (*b*) Explain why a *compiler* makes more efficient use of the processor when compared to an *interpreter* during translation/execution of a loop.　2

   (*c*) *Systematic* and *comprehensive testing* can be used to test progams.

         (i) State the meaning of **systematic** testing.　1

         (ii) State the meaning of **comprehensive** testing.　1

(60)

[Turn over

[END OF SECTION II]

[BLANK PAGE]

SECTION III

Attempt one sub-section of Section III.

For the sub-section chosen, attempt *all* questions.

SECTION III   *Marks*

PART A — Artificial Intelligence

Attempt all questions.

23. Computers have had success playing games against human opponents. Chess is an example of one such game.

(*a*) State **one** characteristic of chess that makes it suitable for computers to play.   1

(*b*) Some people would argue that a chess computer is an example of *artificial intelligence*.

    (i) State **one** definition of artificial intelligence.   1

    (ii) State **one** argument to support the view that the chess computer exhibits artificial intelligence.   1

    (iii) State **one** argument against the view that the chess computer is artificially intelligent.   1

(*c*) In chess, white plays first and can make one of twenty possible moves; black can then make one of twenty possible moves. Explain how the term *combinatorial explosion* applies to the game of chess.   1

(*d*) A search technique uses an evaluation function in order to identify more promising nodes.

    (i) State the search technique being used.   1

    (ii) Describe **one** advantage of this search technique over other search techniques.   2

SECTION III

Marks

PART A — Artificial Intelligence (continued)

24. The paragraph below contains some information about spiders.

> Spiders have eight legs. They have both silk and venom.
>
> Black Widow and Huntsman are types of spider.
>
> Huntsman spiders have eight eyes.

This knowledge is represented graphically as:

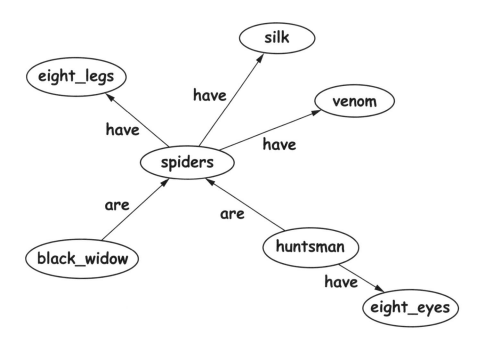

(*a*) (i) State the **name** of this graphical technique for representing knowledge.   1

(ii) State **one** reason why this knowledge representation technique aids the implementation in a declarative language.   1

(*b*) (i) Use the information in the diagram above to state **one** fact using Prolog or similar.   2

(ii) Both the Huntsman and the Black Widow have eight legs. Write **one** rule so that they *inherit* this property.   3

(iii) State **one** benefit of using an *inheritance* rule.   1

[Turn over

SECTION III

Marks

PART A — Artificial Intelligence (continued)

25. Matches is a puzzle where twenty-four matches are arranged into three bundles of eleven, ten and three.

  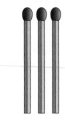

| | 11 matches | 10 matches | 3 matches |

The object of the puzzle is to create the goal state of three **equal** bundles of eight matches.

8 matches　　　　8 matches　　　　8 matches

Matches must be transferred from one bundle to another so that:

- the number of matches in the receiving bundle is **doubled**
- there is **at least** one match in the original bundle.

(a) The initial state of the puzzle could be represented as (11, 10, 3). Use this notation to write down the *goal state*.　　　**1**

(b) One possible move would be to take ten matches from the left bundle and place them on the middle in order to **double** the middle bundle to twenty. This is represented in a search tree as:

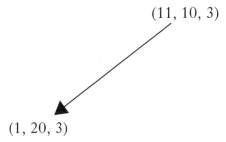

(11, 10, 3)

(1, 20, 3)

(i) State the next **two** nodes in this tree that would be generated using a *breadth-first search*.　　　**2**

(ii) State the next **two** nodes that could be generated using a *depth-first search* from the node (1, 20, 3).　　　**2**

(iii) State **one** advantage of breadth-first compared to depth-first.　　　**1**

(c) Explain how *parallel processing* could improve the speed of finding the goal state in this problem.　　　**2**

SECTION III

Marks

PART A — Artificial Intelligence (continued)

26. A knowledge base contains the following information on Scottish mountains.

1 munro(benmacdui, cairngorms, 1309).   Ben MacDui is a Munro in the Cairngorms. It is 1309 metres high.
2 munro(cairntoul, cairngorms, 1291).
3 munro(bennevis, grampians, 1344).
4 munro(blaven, cuillins, 928).

5 higher(A,B)   IF munro(A,__,P) AND   Munro A is higher than Munro B if Munro A is of height P and
                     munro(B,__,R) AND   Munro B is of height R and
                     P>R.   P is greater than R. We ignore the variable at the underscore.

(*a*) State the solution to the following query:

? munro(A, cuillins, B).

2

(*b*) Use the line numbers to trace the solution to the following query as far as the **first** solution.

? higher(A, B).

In your answer you will be given credit for the correct use of the term *backtrack*.

6

(*c*) Explain what is meant by *instantiation* when evaluating a query.

1

[Turn over

SECTION III

Marks

PART A — Artificial Intelligence (continued)

27. An expert system is used to diagnose different diseases of a patient's respiratory system. The expert system contains rules. Part of one rule is shown below.

> IF the severity of obstruction of the airways IS greater than or equal to mild AND
> the degree of diffusion defect of the patient IS greater
> the TLC observed/predicted of the patient
> the observed/predicted difference in R
> THEN there is evidence that the sub

(*a*)   (i) State the component of the expert system in which this rule would be found.   **1**

    (ii) Describe **two** ways in which justification could be used in a consultation.   **2**

   (iii) State **one** benefit of including a *justification* facility.   **1**

(*b*) One criticism of the expert system is that is has a *narrow domain*.

    (i) Describe what is meant by the term "narrow domain".   **1**

    (ii) Explain **one** benefit of a narrow domain.   **1**

   (iii) State **one** other disadvantage of an expert system when compared to a human expert.   **1**

(*c*) Users complained that the expert system is giving wrong advice in some situations. It is decided to alter some of the rules.

    (i) State the **type** of *maintenance* being undertaken.   **1**

    (ii) Explain why the maintenance of an expert system is difficult.   **2**

SECTION III

Marks

PART A — Artificial Intelligence (continued)

28. A journalist uses a mobile phone application to translate sentences into other languages. The journalist speaks into the phone and the sentence is displayed in English. The phone then translates the sentence into a language chosen by the journalist.

    (a) The journalist says the following sentence:

    > I don't know how mature people enjoy such a show.

    The phone displays:

    > I don't know how much your people enjoy such a show.

        (i) Describe how *speech recognition* is used to identify the words from the digitised sound captured by the microphone. **2**

        (ii) State **one** reason for the mistaken identification of the sentence. **1**

    (b) The phone correctly identifies the following sentence:

    > Charges dropped in submarine attack.

    Explain why the application might have difficulties **interpreting** this sentence. **2**

    (c) The phone can also speak the translated phrase back to the journalist. Name this stage of natural language processing. **1**

    (d) Other than automatic translation, state **one** other application of natural language processing. **1**

    (50)

[END OF SECTION III—PART A]

[Turn over

SECTION III

Marks

PART B — Computer Networking

Attempt all questions.

29. Computers within a hospital are connected together using a computer network.

    (a) Hospital staff are given a username and password to allow them to securely logon to the network. Describe **two** other **software** methods of providing security for the hospital network.

    2

    (b) The hospital network operates using *circuit switching*.

        (i) Describe "circuit switching".

        2

        (ii) The use of *packet switching* could provide several benefits to the hospital network. Describe **one** benefit of packet switching.

        2

        (iii) A network uses *CSMA/CD*. Describe **two** functions of CSMA/CD.

        2

    (c) The hospital network uses *TCP/IP* to transfer files across the network.

        (i) State **three** operations of the **TCP** part of this protocol.

        3

        (ii) State **two** operations of the **IP** part of this protocol.

        2

        (iii) Name **one** other common protocol that could be used to transfer files across the hospital network.

        1

    (d) A nurse tries to access the hospital network from his home computer using the correct login details. The following error message is displayed.

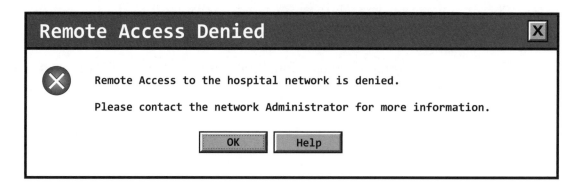

    State **one** reason why this error message would have been displayed.

    1

SECTION III

Marks

PART B — Computer Networking (continued)

29. **(continued)**

(e) The hospital has a website. Some of the web pages can be accessed from WAP enabled devices. These web pages are written using *WML*. The WML code below is entered into a text editor.

```
<wml>
    <card id="Card" title="Doctor Details">
    <p>Dr Smith</p>
</wml>
```

Identify the error in the above WML code.

1

[Turn over

SECTION III

Marks

PART B — Computer Networking (continued)

30. I-Play is an online games company. The I-Play website can be found using a search engine.

(a) Below are two descriptions of methods used by search engines to build their indexes. Name **each** of the methods.

    (i) "Finds pages by following the links in webpages and adding them to their search engine indexes."   **1**

    (ii) "Passes queries on to several search engines and then summarises all the results."   **1**

(b) Describe the purpose of the *Domain Name Service* (DNS) when a customer tries to access the I-Play website.   **2**

In the past, when a customer purchased a game from the I-Play website a CD-ROM was sent out by post. However, customers are now able to download games direct from the I-Play website.

(c) State **one** benefit of allowing customers to download the games.   **1**

(d) A 200 megabyte game is downloaded in 3 minutes. Calculate the transfer rate used to download this game. Express your answer in megabits per second and to 1 decimal place. Show all working.   **2**

(e) Multi-player games are available to play on the website. There is a criticism that these games could make players socially isolated. Explain **one** reason why this might not be the case.   **2**

(f) I-Play is worried that its computer network may develop faults, causing its website to become inaccessible to its users. Name and describe **two** *disaster avoidance* techniques to help prevent its network from breaking down.   **4**

(g) I-Play is also worried about threats to its network security, in particular *passive* and *active attacks*.

    (i) Describe an example of a passive attack that could take place on I-Play's network.   **1**

    (ii) Describe an example of an active attack that could take place on I-Play's network.   **1**

    (iii) Explain why I-Play would find it difficult to detect a passive attack.   **1**

SECTION III

Marks

PART B — Computer Networking (continued)

30. **(continued)**

(*h*) An I-Play customer sets up a *WPAN* between some of his devices. Each device is configured and working correctly and has the required hardware and software installed. However, some of the devices will not connect to this network. State **one** reason why the devices might not connect.

1

(*i*) An I-Play customer has recently upgraded their Internet connection from ISDN to ADSL. State **two** benefits that the customer will gain from upgrading to an ADSL connection.

2

[Turn over

SECTION III

Marks

PART B — Computer Networking (continued)

31. A local tax office has 300 computers connected together in a Local Area Network with access to the Internet.

    (a) The network conforms to the *Open Systems Interconnection (OSI) model.*

        (i) State which **layer** of the OSI model carries out **encryption**.   1

        (ii) State which **layer** of the OSI model carries out **routing**.   1

    (b) Explain which class of IP address is most appropriate for the tax office to use to network their computers.   2

    (c) A former employee attempts a *Denial of Service (DOS)* attack on the tax office.

        (i) Name and describe **one** type of DOS attack that the former employee could have attempted.   2

        (ii) Explain **one** reason why this DOS attack might succeed despite the correct installation of a firewall and anti-virus software.   2

    (d) Due to the DOS attack, the police are now investigating the network usage of the tax office. Explain how The Regulation of Investigatory Powers Act would help the police carry out this investigation.   2

    (e) The tax office has a website which offers advice and support to clients. One webpage contains the text "Tax Calculator". This text is **centred** and is in **bold**.

    Write the HTML code required for this line of text.   3

SECTION III

Marks

PART B — Computer Networking (continued)

31. (continued)

(*f*) This photograph is to be added to the above web page.

Explain why the web designer has chosen to store the image as a JPEG.   2

(50)

[END OF SECTION III—PART B]

[Turn over

SECTION III

Marks

PART C — Multimedia Technology

Attempt all questions.

32. A task to create an interactive presentation is given as part of a multimedia course.

> ## Multimedia Course Task
>
> • Create an interactive presentation to guide new students around the college.
>
> • Your presentation must include the sound files and video clips provided.
>
> • The completed presentation must be submitted as a single file.

(a) (i) Name **one** technique that could be used to design the presentation. 1

(ii) State **one** feature or item that should be included in the design. 1

(b) WYSIWYG allows students to see what their slides look like as they are created. State **one** other benefit of using WYSIWYG during the creation of slides. 1

(c) The presentation will make use of a computer's graphics and sound cards. Graphics and sound cards have a *Digital Signal Processor (DSP)*. State **two** purposes of a DSP. 2

(d) Several of the sound files provided are in the *MIDI file format*. A student decides to edit the attributes of a MIDI file.

(i) Describe the effect on a note of increasing the value of the *duration* attribute. 1

(ii) Describe the effect on a sound of increasing the value of the *tempo* attribute. 1

(e) One of the sound files has two channels but one channel is much louder and is drowning out the other. Name a **technique** that could be used to correct this problem. 1

(f) Name and describe **one** method which students could use to submit their completed presentation as a **single** file. 2

SECTION III

Marks

PART C — Multimedia Technology (continued)

33. A new logo has been designed for the Summit Walking Club. The logo has been stored in *SVG*, *JPEG* and *GIF* file formats.

(*a*) Explain why **SVG** is a suitable file format for this logo.   2

(*b*) The **GIF** and **JPEG** versions of the logo are placed onto a photograph to produce the images below.

Image A

Image B

State which image uses the **GIF** version. State **one** reason for your answer.   2

(*c*) *Interlacing* is supported by the GIF file format. Explain the effect of interlacing when an image is displayed on a web page.   2

[Turn over

SECTION III   *Marks*

PART C — Multimedia Technology (continued)

33. **(continued)**

(*d*) Image C shows an enlarged area of the GIF logo and the effect of *dithering*.

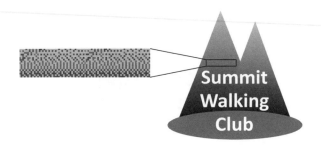

Image C

    (i) Explain the technique of dithering.   2

    (ii) State why dithering is often used with the GIF file format.   1

(*e*) The GIF file format stores a *CLUT* along with the image.

    (i) State the purpose of a CLUT.   1

    (ii) Describe **one** benefit given by the use of a CLUT.   1

(*f*) Both the JPEG and GIF file formats feature *compression*.

    (i) The JPEG file format uses the *RLE* technique. Describe the RLE
technique.   2

    (ii) The GIF file format used the *LZW* technique. Describe the LZW
technique.   2

(*g*) One colour used in the logo can be represented using the *RGB* colour code **(80, 80, 80)**.

    (i) Explain how an RGB colour code represents a colour.   1

    (ii) Describe the effect of editing the code to **(80, 80, 190)**.   1

    (iii) Each part of the RGB code is represented as an 8 bit binary number.
State the number of different colours which can be represented in RGB
code.   1

SECTION III

Marks

PART C — Multimedia Technology (continued)

34. Jakub plays in a band. The band often uses a digital sound recorder during rehearsals.

(a) The uncompressed file size of a 24 bit stereo recording sampled at 88·2 KHz is 60 Mb. Calculate the time that the file plays for. Show all working. State your answer to the nearest second.

3

(b) State **one** benefit of the digital sound recorder having a *memory card reader* rather than internal *solid state storage*.

1

(c) Explain why the digital sound recorder requires an *ADC*.

2

(d) The digital sound recorder can store files in either *WAV* or *MP3* file format. Explain why the band may prefer to listen to recorded sound stored in the WAV file format rather than MP3 file format.

2

(e) Jakub has a *surround sound* system at home. Explain why Jakub may notice little difference between recordings played on his surround sound system and other stereo systems.

2

(f) (i) Jakub usually uses *WiFi* to transfer a video clip from his phone to the drummer's phone. State **two** reasons why Jakub uses WiFi for this transfer.

2

(ii) While rehearsing in a games hall, Jakub has no WiFi access. State **one other** wireless standard that Jakub could use. Justify your choice.

2

(g) Jakub has a video clip taken using his phone. The 60 second video was recorded at 15 fps using a bit depth of 16 bits and a resolution of 640 × 360. Calculate the uncompressed file size for this video clip to the nearest megabyte. Show all working.

3

[Turn over

SECTION III

Marks

PART C — Multimedia Technology (continued)

35. Ms Masters is teaching her class about using *vector file formats* to store graphics. She tells the class "Vector graphic file formats are more storage efficient than bit-mapped file formats".

   (*a*) Describe the type of graphic Ms Masters might use to show that the statement above is true.   1

   (*b*) Describe what happens to a vector graphic in order for it to be displayed on a monitor.   1

The class are instructed to draw a *3D* object, apply a *texture* and store it in a vector graphic file format.

   (*c*) Explain the term "texture" when applied to a **3D** object.   1

   (*d*) Name **one** possible *attribute* required to store a 3D object **in addition** to those attributes required to store a 2D object.   1

   (*e*) Name a file format suitable for storing a 3D vector graphic image.   1

(50)

[*END OF SECTION III—PART C*]

[*END OF QUESTION PAPER*]

HIGHER

2014

HODDER
GIBSON
LEARN MORE

[BLANK PAGE]

X206/12/01

NATIONAL
QUALIFICATIONS
2014

FRIDAY, 23 MAY
9.00 AM – 11.30 AM

COMPUTING
HIGHER

Attempt **all** questions in Section I.

Attempt **all** questions in Section II.

Attempt **one** sub-section of Section III.

Part A	Artificial Intelligence	Page 12	Questions 24 to 27
Part B	Computer Networking	Page 19	Questions 28 to 30
Part C	Multimedia Technology	Page 25	Questions 31 to 34

For the sub-section chosen, attempt **all** questions.

Read all questions carefully.

Do not write on the question paper.

Write as neatly as possible.

SECTION I   *Marks*

Attempt all questions in this section.

1. Convert this 8 bit *two's complement* binary number into its decimal equivalent.
    11001110.   1

2. *Unicode* and *ASCII* can both be used to represent characters.
    Describe **one advantage** of Unicode over ASCII.   1

3. This line has been created using a *vector graphics* package.

    State **two** attributes that are required to store this line.   2

4. One *purpose of a register* is to hold *an instruction to be executed*.
    State **one** other item that can be held in a register.   1

5. Name the term used to describe the concept of each memory location being identified
    by a unique binary number.   1

6. *Solid state storage devices* contain no moving parts and are more robust than external
    hard disk drives.
    Describe **two** other reasons for using solid state storage instead of an external hard
    disk drive.   2

7. One *function of an interface* is to convert a continuous temperature signal to a *digital*
    signal. Name this function.   1

8. State **one** function of a *web server*.   1

SECTION I (continued)

Marks

9. Describe the function of a *bootstrap loader*.   1

10. State the type of system software of which a *disk editor* is an example.   1

11. Tian's computer is infected with a virus that is activated within a general purpose package.

    (a) State the *type of virus* that has attacked the system.   1

    (b) Describe how a *checksum* could be used to detect a virus.   2

12. The software development process is described as an *iterative* process.

    Use an example to explain how the production of the software specification is an iterative process.   2

13. An App has been created which calculates the amount of annual interest earned on the money in a bank account. Here is the top level algorithm, including data flow for steps 1 and 3.

    1. get amount in bank and interest rate   (out: amount, out: rate)

    2. calculate annual interest   . . . .

    3. display annual interest   (in: interest)

    (a) State which design notation is being used.   1

    (b) State **one** parameter, and its data flow, which is required at step 2.   1

14. During the implementation stage programmers may make use of a *module library*.

    State **two** reasons why the use of a module library improves development time.   2

[Turn over

Marks

SECTION I (continued)

15. After software is written it must be evaluated against various criteria.

    (*a*) Name the criterion being described below:

    "program does not make unnecessary use of system resources such as RAM".   **1**

    (*b*) Name the criterion being described below:

    "program will run on other computer systems and operating systems with minimal changes required".   **1**

16. Many applications contain *scripting* languages which allow the creation of macros.

    State **one** benefit of using macros within an application.   **1**

17. A program may make use of a 1–D array.

    (*a*) When declaring a 1–D array for use in a program, the array must be given a name.

    State **two** other items which should be specified when the array is declared.   **2**

    (*b*) Explain why it is more *efficient* in terms of its use of system resources to pass an array *by reference* rather than *by value*.   **2**

18. Software development companies employ *independent test groups* during the testing stage. These are made up of people who are **not** part of the software development company or employed by the client.

    State **two** reasons why the software development company uses an independent test group.   **2**

    (30)

[END OF SECTION I]

SECTION II

Marks

Attempt all questions in this section.

19. Michael is a personal fitness trainer and uses a computer to create and print leaflets that will advertise his classes.

    (*a*) When creating the leaflets Michael can make use of either *bit mapped graphics* or *vector graphics*.

        (i) State **one** advantage of using bit mapped graphics over vector graphics.   1

        (ii) Other than file size, state **one** advantage of using vector graphics over bit mapped graphics.   1

    (*b*) When printing the leaflets, Michael's computer system may make use of *spooling*.

    Describe how spooling operates during printing.   2

    (*c*) Michael recommends a piece of software that will guide his clients through exercises that can be completed at home.

    Describe **two** *hardware compatibility issues* that his clients will have to consider before installing the software.   2

    (*d*) Part of the software allows users to update a daily diary after each training session.

    The *Memory Management* function of the operating system will allocate and de-allocate memory addresses as the diary is edited.

    Describe **two** roles of *Memory Management* during the process of **saving** the diary to backing storage.   2

    (*e*) Name the law that makes the unauthorised distribution of software illegal.   1

[Turn over

SECTION II (continued)

Marks

20. Katerina runs a small business offering Internet access within an airport coffee shop. Each computer in the coffee shop is connected to a network.

    Katerina has decided to use a *ring topology* to structure the network.

    (a) Draw a **labelled** diagram of a ring topology.

    2

    For security reasons Katerina needs to take a photograph of each member of staff. Katerina uploads the files from her camera to a computer on the network.

    (b) *Handling Status Signals* is one function of an interface involved in this data transfer.

    State **two** examples of status signals that the interface may have to handle when the data is transferred from Katerina's camera to the computer.

    2

    (c) The camera is connected to the computer via a *serial* interface.

    Explain why serial transmission can be described as more reliable than *parallel transmission*.

    1

    (d) Katerina downloaded a file to her laptop computer on Monday. She downloaded the same file to her desktop computer on Wednesday. She used both computers to access her online banking service during the following week. Both computers began to show symptoms of a virus within an hour of the banking access. The computer in the bank does **not** have a virus.

    Name and describe the *virus code action* that is demonstrated here.

    2

    (e) Katerina is also concerned that the network may be subject to an attack from a *worm* or a *Trojan horse*.

    Explain why Katerina might be more concerned about an attack from a worm rather than a Trojan.

    2

SECTION II (continued) *Marks*

21. JCN manufacture tablet computers. Yusif has recently started work with JCN. He is working on the development of processors for a new tablet computer.

    (a) Some processors contain *cache memory*. Explain how cache memory can improve system performance. **2**

    (b) Yusif has learned that processors have to perform *memory write* operations.

    Describe the steps in a memory write operation. Your answer should make reference to the appropriate *buses* and *control lines*. **4**

    (c) Yusif has been asked to design a tablet computer that can support a **maximum** addressable memory of 64Gb. He has been told that the *address bus* width will be 32 lines.

    Calculate the number of lines required for the *data bus*. **3**

    (d) Yusif is to measure the performance of a tablet computer. He will use FLOPS to measure the performance of the processor.

        (i) Explain why Yusif may choose to measure processor performance using FLOPS. **2**

        (ii) Explain why Yusif **would not** use *application based tests* as a measure of processor performance. **1**

[Turn over

SECTION II (continued)

Marks

22. Garthaven Council want a booking system, for use within the council offices, to assist with the booking of evening classes and activities. They employ LetUsWriteIt, a software development company, to write the software.

    (a) Mark, the systems analyst, interviews council staff to try to find out exactly what is required within the system.

    State **two** difficulties which Mark may encounter when using interviews to aid the analysis.   2

    (b) When designing the structure and logic of a program, *top-down design* is used.

    Explain what is meant by "top-down design".   1

    (c) It is decided that the user interface should look similar to the one shown below.

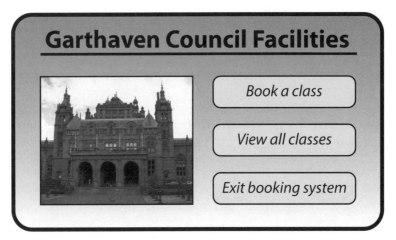

    An *event driven language* is used to implement this software.

    State **two** reasons why an event driven language has been chosen.   2

    (d) A team of programmers start to create the code.

    Explain **one** way the team can efficiently work together to create the code.   2

    (e) The programmers carry out *systematic testing*.

    State what is meant by the term systematic testing.   1

    (f) The final version of the software is translated using a compiler and the compiled code is distributed to other offices.

    Explain why the compiled code is distributed, rather than the program code.   2

SECTION II (continued)   *Marks*

22. **(continued)**

(g) State **two** characteristics of well written code which will help during *maintenance* of software.   2

(h) Garthaven Council would now like the booking system to be made available as an App for use by residents.

State **two** reasons why *portability* of software is an important factor for developers to consider.   2

(i) After several months, the Council decide that they would like to include a "manage a booking" option.

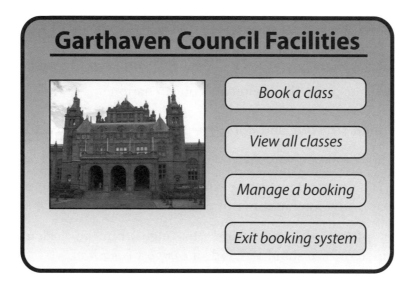

Name the **type** of maintenance needed to include this feature in the software.

Justify your answer.   2

[Turn over

SECTION II (continued)   *Marks*

23. A sci-fi fan club allows its members to buy reduced price tickets for national events.

A program is written to store, search and sort member details and to create IDs.

A few of the fan club members' details are shown below.

ID	Email	Region
WalkJa	Jwalker12@basics.com	West
BrowHa	BrownH2@vmail.com	East
KhanSy	Jedi34@wmail.com	North
SmitAl	R2D3@mymail.com	West
HarvSa	C3P7@jmail.com	North

and so on . . .

(a) Jack Walker was assigned the ID "WalkJa" using *concatenation*.

Explain what is meant by the term "concatenation".   1

(b) State the *data structure* and *data type* which could be used to store the **list** of IDs.   2

(c) An event is being held involving both the East and West regions. The fan club needs to know the total number of people who could be involved.

   (i) Use *pseudocode* to design an algorithm to calculate this total. Your algorithm should include a *complex condition*.   5

   (ii) The algorithm is to be amended to display the contact e-mail for the East and West members.

   State the line to be added and indicate where it should be placed in the algorithm.   2

   (iii) The program could be amended to count the number of members in each individual region.

   Name a programming construct that uses *multiple outcome selection* to implement this.   1

(d) The program uses *global* variables.

   (i) State the *scope* of a global variable.   1

   (ii) State **two** benefits of using parameter passing rather than global variables when programming.   2

    (60)

[END OF SECTION II]

SECTION III

Attempt one sub-section of Section III.

For the sub-section chosen, attempt *all* questions.

[Turn over

SECTION III   *Marks*

PART A — Artificial Intelligence

Attempt all questions.

24. Two schools are taking part in a competition based on the Turing Test. The competition involves creating software capable of a realistic conversation with a human judge. Niall is the human judge and he will have to determine whether he is communicating with the school system or a human.

Niall will enter text using the keyboard and see responses on his monitor.

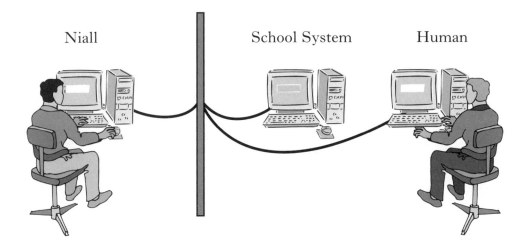

Annebank Academy is one of the two schools. Their school's system is a *chatterbot* based on *Eliza*.

(a) Explain how the chatterbot will generate a response to Niall.   3

(b) Niall decides to use a grammatically incorrect sentence as a strategy for identifying which is the Annebank chatterbot and which is the human. He types:

Cinema to the I went.

Explain how the incorrect grammar would affect the chatterbot's response.   2

(c) The other school, Straiton High School, has created a system based on *Natural Language Processing* (NLP).

  (i) Name and describe the stage of Natural Language Processing that will process the typed input.   2

  (ii) Name the other stage of Natural Language Processing that would be part of this system.   1

SECTION III

Marks

PART A — Artificial Intelligence (continued)

24. **(continued)**

    (d) Natural Language Processing can encounter difficulties even though Niall is typing his responses instead of speaking them.

    State **one** such difficulty using an example to illustrate your point.

    2

    (e) Niall could use other strategies to identify whether he is communicating with the school system or the human.

    Explain **one** other strategy that Niall could use in the identification.

    1

    (f) When creating the software the schools chose between declarative and procedural languages. Other than the use of procedures, state **two** features of procedural languages that differ from declarative languages.

    2

[Turn over

SECTION III

Marks

PART A — Artificial Intelligence (continued)

25. Artificial neural systems (ANS) are used in medicine for diagnosis. They use inputs such as gender, heart rate and blood count.

    (*a*) The *domain* for an ANS used in medical diagnosis would need to be restricted.

    Describe **two** ways in which the domain could be restricted. 2

    (*b*) Describe how *layers* are used in an ANS. 1

    (*c*) (i) Explain why the *weights* in an artificial neuron are altered during learning. 2

    (ii) In addition to weights, state another value in an artificial neuron which may be altered during learning. 1

    (iii) Explain why the learning process of an ANS is iterative. 1

    (*d*) Explain how *parallel processing* could improve the performance of an ANS. 2

    (*e*) Artificial neural systems demonstrate aspects of intelligence such as the ability to learn.

    State **two** other aspects of intelligence. 2

SECTION III

Marks

PART A — Artificial Intelligence (continued)

26. The Towers of Hanoi is a puzzle that can be solved using search techniques. The object of the puzzle is to move a set of discs from one peg to another. Only one disc can be moved at a time and a larger disc cannot be placed on a smaller disc.

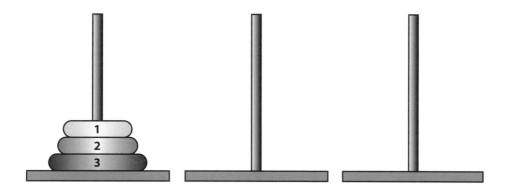

In this version of the puzzle the large disc is numbered 3, the middle size disc is 2 and the smallest disc is 1.

The *start state* of the puzzle is shown in the diagram above and can be represented using the notation.

$$[(3,2,1),(\ ),(\ )]$$

(a) The puzzle is solved when the *goal state* shown below is reached.

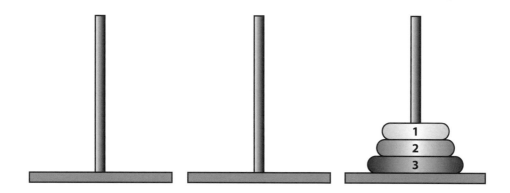

Use the same notation to represent the goal state shown above.   1

[Turn over

SECTION III

Marks

PART A — Artificial Intelligence (continued)

26. **(continued)**

    (b) A *depth-first search* is being used to find a solution.

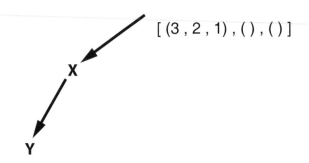

Copy and complete the search tree above showing **one** possible missing node at **each of** X and Y for the depth-first search.

2

    (c) Explain why a depth-first search could be more efficient than a breadth-first search.

2

    (d) (i) A node can be represented as [(2 , 1) , ( ) , (3)]. Copy and complete the diagram below indicating the position of the discs for this node.

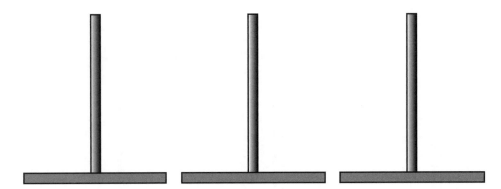

1

        (ii) From this state, write down the missing two states leading to the goal state.

[(2 , 1) , ( ) , (3)]	[?]	[?]	[( ) , ( ) , (3 , 2 , 1)]

2

SECTION III

Marks

PART A — Artificial Intelligence (continued)

26. **(continued)**.

(e) A *heuristic search technique* can reduce search times when puzzles result in *combinatorial explosion*.

   (i) Explain how a heuristic search technique can reduce search times.

2

  (ii) Explain why *combinatorial explosion* is not a problem for this puzzle.

2

 (iii) Other than parallel processing, state **one** improvement in hardware that could improve search times.

1

[Turn over

SECTION III

Marks

PART A — Artificial Intelligence (continued)

27. A knowledge base contains some information about the human body.

    1. is_part(inner_ear,ear).   *The inner ear is part of the ear.*
    2. is_part(middle_ear,ear).
    3. is_part(outer_ear,ear).
    4. is_part(cerebellum,brain).

    5. is_part(cochlea,inner_ear).
    6. is_part(vestibular,inner_ear).
    7. is_part(eardrum,middle_ear).
    8. is_part(ossicles,middle_ear).

    9. function_of(balance,inner_ear).   *Balance is a function of the inner ear.*
    10. function_of(sound_transfer,middle_ear).
    11. function_of(movement,cerebellum).
    12. function_of (balance, cerebellum)

    13. located_in(A, B) IF is_part(A, B).   *A is located in B if A is part of B.*

    14. located_in(A, B) IF is_part(A, C)   *A is located in B if A is part of C*
        AND located_in(C, B).   *AND C is located in B.*

    (*a*) State the solutions to the following query:

        ? is_part(A, middle_ear)   2

    (*b*) State the query that would be entered to ask the question:

        What is the function of the cerebellum?   2

    (*c*) Use the line numbers to trace the following query as far as the **second** solution.

        ? located_in(ossicles, B)

        In your answer you will be given credit for the correct use of the term *sub-goal*.   7

    (*d*) Explain what is meant by *backtracking* in the evaluation of a query.   2

                                                                                    (50)

[END OF SECTION III—PART A]

SECTION III   *Marks*

PART B — Computer Networking

Attempt all questions.

28. FunPark is a new theme park in Scotland. All ticket booths are connected to the central network server.

The server also hosts the FunPark website and manages e-mail.

(*a*) Several *protocols* are used by this network. State which protocol should be used for each of the purposes below.

   (i) A sales person sending an e-mail to their manager.   **1**

   (ii) The manager uploading photos to the web server.   **1**

   (iii) A customer accessing the FunPark website.   **1**

(*b*) The IP address of a computer in one of the ticket booths is:

                            178.21.8.245

State the *class* of this IP address. Justify your answer.   **2**

(*c*) The network manager adds a new computer to the network and allocates this IP address:

                            172.21.6.247

An error message is displayed.

State **one** reason why this IP address is incorrect.   **1**

(*d*) The FunPark website has the address www.funpark.com.

When a customer enters the address into a browser, it is sent to a *domain name server* (DNS) to be resolved.

Describe what happens during a successful *domain name resolution*.   **2**

SECTION III

Marks

PART B — Computer Networking (continued)

28. (continued)

(e) Unexpected weather has caused the theme park to close.

The webpage shown has to be added to the website.

It has the title "Park Closed" and displays two lines of text.

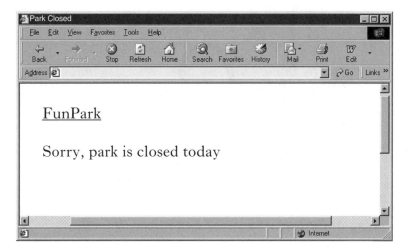

Copy and complete the table, showing the *HTML* code that is required for this webpage.

<html>
<p>Sorry, park is closed today</p>
</html>

4

SECTION III

Marks

PART B — Computer Networking (continued)

28. **(continued)**

(*f*) The FunPark website was created using HTML and cannot be displayed on some mobile phones.

The website is re-written using WML.

(i) Name the protocol that must be used to allow the WML website to be viewed on mobile phones.   1

(ii) Explain why the re-writing of the website code is an example of *adaptive maintenance*.   1

(iii) Describe **one** feature of WML that differs from HTML.   1

(*g*) A customer uses a *meta-search engine* to search for the FunPark website.

Describe how a meta-search engine would find the FunPark website.   2

(*h*) The home page of the FunPark website includes the following HTML code:

<meta name= "keywords" content="FunPark Scotland Theme Park Rollercoaster"/>

State the search engine method that would use this line of code and explain what the code is used for.   2

[Turn over

SECTION III   *Marks*

PART B — Computer Networking (continued)

29. Aimee works in a local branch of a multi-national bank. All of the computers in the branch are linked to a Wide Area Network.

(a) Part of Aimee's job is to update customer files. However, when opening a file, the error message "Access Denied" is displayed.

Error: Access Denied
Current User   **You are signed in as : Aimee Munro**
Contact your network administrator for further assistance

Describe what the network administrator should do to allow Aimee to open this file.   1

(b) The bank is concerned about *passive* and *active* network security attacks. Describe **two** examples of active attacks that could take place within the bank network.   2

(c) Data is transferred around the bank's network using *asynchronous data transmission*.

   (i) Describe asynchronous data transmission.   2

   (ii) Explain **one** way in which asynchronous data transmission could **decrease** network performance.   2

(d) The *TCP/IP* protocol is used within the bank network when transmitting data.

   (i) State **two** operations carried out by the TCP part of the protocol.   2

   (ii) State **one** operation carried out by the IP part of the protocol.   1

(e) Aimee can access the Internet from her work computer. However, Internet access is restricted by *Internet filtering software*.

   (i) State **two** methods that the Internet filtering software would use to restrict Internet access.   2

   (ii) The bank manager thinks that a *walled garden* would be a more suitable method to restrict Internet access.

     Describe how a walled garden would stop access to all unsuitable sites.   1

   (iii) Explain **one** reason why Internet filtering software could not stop access to all unsuitable sites.   1

SECTION III   *Marks*

PART B — Computer Networking (continued)

30. Eldor is a travel agency that has many branches nationwide.

   (*a*) Eldor's computer network uses a *packet switched* network rather than a *circuit switched* network.

      (i) Describe what happens to the packets when data is being transferred over the packet switched network.   2

      (ii) Other than cost, explain **one** advantage of packet switching over circuit switching for the Eldor network.   2

   (*b*) A sales representative uses a *Wireless Personal Area Network* (WPAN) to connect his laptop, mobile phone and tablet computer together. These devices could have been connected using Eldor's *Wireless Local Area Network* (WLAN).

      State **two** differences between a WPAN and a WLAN.   2

   (*c*) All computers linked to the Eldor network use the Open Systems Interconnection (OSI) Model.

      Each device on the network has a network interface card which has its own MAC address.

      (i) State **one** reason why the OSI model was developed.   1

      (ii) Explain why it is necessary for each device on the network to have a unique MAC address.   1

      (iii) Name the layer of the OSI model which makes use of the MAC address.   1

   (*d*) *Parity checks* are carried out on the data being transmitted around the Eldor network.

      (i) The data below has arrived at its destination and a parity error has been found.

Data before being sent	Data at destination
1001 1000	1001 1001

      State which type of parity is being used here. Explain your answer.   2

      (ii) Other than parity, name another method that could be used to detect errors in data transmission.   1

   (*e*) A 25 megabyte file is transferred over the Eldor network in 5 seconds.

      Calculate the transfer rate in megabits per second used to transfer this file. Show all working.   2

SECTION III

Marks

PART B — Computer Networking (continued)

30. (continued)

(*f*) Eldor has a website that allows customers 24 hour access to buy holidays online.

   (i) State **one** benefit to the customer, other than 24 hour access, of buying holidays online.

1

  (ii) Some customers are worried about making online payments when buying holidays online.

      Name two **visual** features that should be displayed on the payment page to show that the website is secure and uses encryption.

2

(50)

[END OF SECTION III—PART B]

SECTION III

Marks

PART C — Multimedia Technology

Attempt all questions.

31. Pupils from a school ICT club have created a website.

   (*a*) The pupils used *authoring software* with a *WYSIWYG* editor and text editor to create the web pages.

     (i) State **one** benefit, other than faster creation, for the pupils in using the WYSIWYG authoring software features.   1

     (ii) State **one** advantage for the pupils in using the text editor to create a web page.   1

   (*b*) Some web pages display differently depending on the browser used.

     State the type of maintenance required to try to correct the differences.   1

     Many web pages in the website contain video clips. Some video clips are *streamed* while others are *embedded*.

   (*c*) Explain **one** advantage of streaming files rather than embedding files.   2

   (*d*) Explain **one** advantage of embedding data when playing video clips.   2

   (*e*) One of the video clips plays for 32 seconds and was recorded at 25 fps. Each frame has a resolution of 1280 x 720 and a colour depth of 24 bits. Calculate the storage requirement for this uncompressed video clip. Write your answer in Gigabytes. Show all working.   3

   (*f*) Many video clips are stored in the MPEG file format.

     Describe how MPEG achieves compression of the video clip.   2

   (*g*) Some of the web pages have links to *synthesised* sound files.

     (i) State the most common file type used to store synthesised sounds.   1

     (ii) Explain why synthesised sounds stored in this file format may play differently when played on different computers.   2

[Turn over

SECTION III   *Marks*

PART C — Multimedia Technology (continued)

32. Helen regularly uses slide shows to present her work. She wants to personalise her slide shows by displaying some text in her handwriting rather than a standard font. Helen uses a scanner to input a handwritten copy of her name. The edges on the first scan look jagged.

(a) Explain how altering the scanner settings could make the edges of the image smoother.   2

(b) Name **one** software technique Helen could also use to try to correct the jagged edges and describe how this technique achieves a smoother image.   2

(c) Helen stores the scanned image in the JPEG file format and inserts the image on a slide.

   (i) Explain why saving the image as a JPEG has resulted in the image being surrounded by a white box as shown.

                                                                          1

   (ii) Name a file format Helen could use to store her scanned image to remove this problem.   1

SECTION III

Marks

PART C — Multimedia Technology (continued)

32. **(continued)**

(d) Helen would like to animate her image.

Name a file format suitable for storing animated graphics. **1**

(e) Helen uses her digital camera to take photographs for inclusion in her presentations.

Digital cameras and scanners both use CCDs to capture images.

Explain the difference in how the CCDs in a digital camera and a scanner are arranged. **2**

(f) Helen considers creating a font based on her handwriting. Fonts can be stored using a *vector graphic* or *bitmapped* file format.

(i) Explain why a vector file format might be preferred to a bitmapped file format when storing a font. **2**

(ii) Explain **one** reason why some fonts might be stored in bitmapped file format. **1**

[Turn over

SECTION III

Marks

PART C — Multimedia Technology (continued)

33. Image A was stored as a 2D vector graphic. It was then altered to be in 3D.

Image A   Image B

(*a*) Name **two** additional attributes that are required to be able to create the 3D representation shown in image B.

2

(*b*) Name a suitable file format for the 3D image.

1

(*c*) 3D imaging has become more popular in recent years.

State **two** hardware developments, other than increased storage capacity, which have contributed to this.

2

(*d*) Research into holographic storage has continued due to the demand for increased storage capacity in small devices.

State how holographic storage would achieve increased storage capacity.

1

SECTION III   *Marks*

PART C — Multimedia Technology (continued)

34. AQSound is a business which creates sounds for games software.

   (a) Calculate the storage required for an uncompressed 12 second sound which has been created by AQSound at a frequency of 48 kilohertz with a sampling depth of 2 bytes and 6 channels.

   Write your answer in megabytes. Show all working.   **3**

   (b) State the feature of a sound card required to play this sound effect properly.   **1**

   (c) Explain why the use of 6 channels allows more realism than stereo. Your answer should include an example.   **2**

   (d) Many of the sounds are created by AQSound with a *bit rate* of 320 kilobits per second.

   Explain the term bit rate.   **1**

   (e) AQSound do not usually normalise sound files used in a game.

      (i) Describe **one** purpose of normalising sound files.   **1**

      (ii) Describe **one** limitation of normalising sound files.   **1**

   (f) AQSound often use a container file to store sound files for games.

      (i) Describe **one** benefit of storing the sound files in a container file.   **1**

      (ii) Describe **one** possible issue with storing the sound files in a container file.   **1**

   (g) Sound cards include a DAC and a DSP.

      (i) The DAC converts digital data into analogue data. Explain why a sound card has a DAC.   **1**

      (ii) The DSP compresses and decompresses sound files. Describe **two** other tasks performed by the DSP.   **2**

   (h) WAV and MP3 are compressed sound file formats.

      (i) Explain how ADPCM achieves compression in the WAV file format. Your explanation should include an appropriate level of technical detail.   **2**

      (ii) One technique used in the MP3 format is to remove sounds outside the hearing range of humans.

      State **one** other way in which MP3 file sizes are reduced.   **1**

   (50)

[END OF SECTION III—PART C]

[END OF QUESTION PAPER]

Acknowledgements

Permission has been sought from all relevant copyright holders and Hodder Gibson is grateful for the use of the following:
Image © Gilmanshin/Shutterstock.com (2013 page 12);
Image © Collpicto/Shutterstock.com (2013 page 15).

SQA HIGHER COMPUTING
2010–2014

COMPUTING HIGHER
2010

SECTION I

1. -45

2. (*a*) The virus waits until a condition is met
    - before it triggers/is activated/performs its task
    - or example of condition eg Date reached, access to Internet

    (*b*) *Any one from:*
    - Replication
    - Camouflage
    - Delivery

3. • An instruction (to be executed)
    • Data (to be processed)

4. *Any one from:*
    - To store data that has been passed from the computer processor (while it waits for the printer to process it)
    - Acts as a buffer
    - Allows computer processor to carry on with other tasks
    - Any other suitable description

5. 2. Read line is activated **or** Read signal is sent
    4. Instruction is decoded and executed

6. (*a*) • Copyright Designs and Patents Act

    (*b*) *Any one from:*
    - The files he shares are copyrighted
    - Not his files to share
    - He does not have permission to make the copies
    - He only has one licence
    - Financial loss to company as a result of reduced sales
    - Any other suitable

7. *Any one from:*
    - LAN will use dedicated (cable or wireless) media and a WAN will use telecommunication systems
    - LAN media owned by the organisation, WAN owned by communication companies
    - LAN tends to be uniform in its type of connection/cable, WAN tends to use more than one type of transmission medium
    - Any other valid difference with explanation

8. *Any one combination from:*
    - Each connected node on a switch receives full bandwidth – Nodes on a hub share the bandwidth
    - Data sent to single/addressed/required node with switch – A hub broadcasts to all nodes
    - Reduction/avoidance of collisions when using a switch – Use of a hub increases network traffic

9. (*a*) A number with fractional part/floating point number/decimal number

    (*b*) Array of Boolean

10. (*a*) *Any one stage and reason from:*
    - Implementation – Program must be planned to show how program is to be coded
    - Testing – Used to create test data/To help identify errors
    - Evaluation – Design is used to ensure that all requirements in software specification are met
    - Documentation – Design is used as a template for the creation of the technical description of the code
    - Maintenance – Design will be looked at and changed to match the maintenance required

    (*b*) *Any two from:*
    - Breaks problem into smaller problems
    - Continuing to break down sub problems
    - Until they can be solved easily/trivially/simply

11. (*a*) *Any one from:*
    - (Structured) listing
    - Printout/hardcopy of program/source code
    - Source code

    (*b*) *Any one from:*
    - Provides a record of work done (required by project manager/client)
    - Aids maintenance (by keeping a record of changes made)
    - Track staff changes within the development team
    - Accept a purpose of a specific type of documentation, such as purpose of User Guide, Technical Guide, Internal Documentation
    - Any other valid

    (*c*) *Any one from:*
    To give advice on:
    - how the parts of the program work
    - the memory/processor/system requirements/specifications
    - potential software/hardware clashes
    - the version/maintenance history
    - Other valid

12. (*a*) *Any one method and reason/effect from:*
    - If compiled version of program is used, meaning translator is not needed during execution
    - Use of local variables where possible, allowing memory to be reused when it goes out of scope
    - Software is modular/has no unnecessary code/variables, saving on memory used for duplicate/unnecessary code
    - Variable types should be appropriate for data for example using integer as opposed to real to save memory
    - Any other valid method and effect/reason

    (*b*) • Software can run on any other platform/processor/"type of computer" **or** other than the one it was designed for with little or no change

13. *Any one from:*
    - Automate complex or frequently used task
    - Writing macros
    - Customising user interface
    - Increase/extend functionality
    - Any valid response

SECTION II

14. (*a*) Bootstrap loader

    (*b*) (i) • Data format conversion – Converting the photograph data from serial to parallel or vice versa (as used in the computer system)
        • Handling of status signals – The camera will send signals to say it is ready to send data

        (ii) *Any two from:*
        - Voltage conversion
        - Protocol conversion
        - Buffering/data storage
        - Any other valid

    (*c*) (i) *Any two from:*
        - Reduce the file size
        - Fewer bits per pixel
        - Faster download
        - Smaller storage on disk/RAM

(ii) Fewer possible colours available (or any other valid), so poorer quality pictures.

(iii) • $4 \times 6 \times 600 \times 600$ pixels
 • 8640000×16 bits
 • $(= 138240000) = 16.48$ Mb

(d) • Memory management − locates the file in main memory
 • Input/Output − controls the moving of (blocks of) data (between main memory and hard drive)

(e) *Any one from:*
 • Faster access times allows almost instant reviewing of pictures
 • Small and lightweight allowing small camera size
 • No moving parts so silent/robust
 • No moving parts so less battery power required
 • Less battery power so more pictures can be taken on one charge

(f) *Any one from:*
 • JPEG is lossy whereas GIF is lossless
 • GIF only has 256 (8 bit) possible colours, JPEG can have 16.7 million (24 bit)
 • JPEG requires less backing storage or memory than the equivalent GIF, hence is faster to transmit
 • GIFs can be animated whereas JPEGs are not (like any graphic format can only be used within animation)
 • GIFs allow transparency whereas JPEGs don't (because they are a single layer)
 • Other valid

15. (a) • 2^{32} possible locations
 • 64 bits per location
 • $2^{32} \times 64$ bits $= 32$ Gbytes

(b) *Any one from:*
 • Cache has faster access time than main memory speeding up fetching
 • Holds frequently used instructions speeding fetching
 • Wider internal bus speeding up data transfer
 • Physically closer to processor speeding up transfer
 • RAM in cache is made up from fast static RAM rather than slower dynamic RAM speeding access times
 • Holds pre-fetched instructions in cache instead of accessing slower main memory

(c) *Any one from:*
 • Compatibility with the operating system to allow software to run/install
 • Sufficient RAM/memory/Backing Storage/Processor to satisfy minimum program requirements/to enable it to run
 • Any other valid with justification

(d) (i) *Any one from:*
 • MIPS measures processor throughput and are independent of other computer components ie hard disk speed
 • ABTs depend on performance of other components and therefore may rate identical processors differently
 • MIPS measures processor throughput whereas ABTs measure the entire system
 • Other valid answer with explanation

(ii) FLOPS **or** Clock Speed

(e) *Any one from:*
 • Each computer has its own backing storage and does not rely on central server
 • No complex server software to set up so easier to create shared area of peer-to-peer
 • Any other suitable

16. (a) String
 And any one from:
 • "Jun" is textual and must be a string
 • Number data types cannot accept text
 • String operations to be carried out

(b) Substring

(c) Case month of
 When "Jan" − Set month to "01"
 When "Feb" − Set month to "02"

(d) Concatenation

(e) 8 bits per character
 $= 8 * 6 = 48$ bits or 6 bytes

(f) (i) *Any two from:*
 • Follows a sequence of instructions/defined start and end point
 • Use of subprograms/functions
 • Range of variable types
 • Program control using repetition and selection structures
 • Uses arithmetical and logical functions
 • Any other valid

(ii) *Any one from:*
 • Code activated/order of execution assigned to particular user action eg clicking on button
 • Routines/code for handling events
 • Predefined routines for the creation of buttons/windows/forms/etc

(g) *Any two from:*
 • Comment lines/internal documentation to describe code
 • Capitalise/highlight/embolden keywords to increase readability
 • Indentation/blank lines/white space to increase readability
 • Meaningful variable/subroutine/function names describes function of code
 • Modular code/use of procedures/functions
 • Use of parameter passing
 • Use of local variables
 • Any other valid

(h) (i) A variable that can be used/accessed/updated anywhere in a program.

(ii) *Any one from:*
 • Unexpected changes to variables caused by variables with the same name interacting
 • Data flow is unclear which reduces readability
 • RAM assigned to local variables is reused, so more efficient use of memory
 • Any other valid response with explanation

17. (a) *Any two from:*
 • Interpreter will translate the contents of the loops every time they are carried out
 • Compiler will translate the contents of the loops once only
 • Saving processor time by reducing the number of translations

(b) *Any one from:*
 Font, size, style, colour, columns/table/tab, alignment

(c) Perfective

(d) (i) • Number of floors in the building
 • Number of rooms on each floor

(ii) • Passed by value
 • The subprogram only needs to use these values, it should not change them

(e) Set min to first temp in array
Set max to first temp in array

For each temp()
   If temp(current)>max then
      Set max to temp(current)

   If temp(current)<min then
      Set min to temp(current)
   End If
Next temp()

SECTION III

Part A – Artificial Intelligence

18. (a) (i) *Any one from:*
- Machines/computers/programs capable of doing task that would require intelligence if done by human
- Ability of computer to show intelligent behaviour
- Any other valid

   (ii) Turing test

   (iii) *Any one from:*
- A human requires intelligence to play the game so the computer is intelligent if it can play/beat the human
- Games have a restricted rule set and a clear goal so they are easier to program
- Games are able to be expressed as logical rules so can be coded easily
- Any other valid fact with explanation

(b) (i) *Any two from:*
- Learning
- Problem solving skills
- Remember facts/experiences
- Language
- Creativity

   (ii) *Any one (matching answer to part (i))from:*
- Learning new strategies that can be applied in future games
- Problem solving to search for appropriate strategy for different situations that occur
- Remembering previous experience to inform future strategy
- Interpreting of typed or spoken commands to perform actions
- The idea of coping with new situations and/or novel solutions

(c) (i) *Any one from:*
- Different processors evaluate different paths/move) simultaneously
- Several possible moves explored independently at same time

   (ii) *Any one from:*
- With more states held in memory, response time should be faster
- A larger amount of game data/states can be stored improving experience and decision making
- Allowing more moves to be stored more complex games can be played
- Valid point leading to improved performance

19. (a) *Any one from:*
- Both systems take a number of inputs
- The strengths of the inputs are totalled
- Both systems use weightings (to boost or inhibit signals)
- If the total value of inputs in each system is greater than a threshold value the neuron fires

(b) • Alter weights
- Alter threshold values

(c) (i) Containing knowledge about a specialised/narrow area eg character recognition, weather forecasting

   (ii) *Any one from:*
- Large known data set or large set of examples for which the output can be given
- Finite set of characteristics for inputs
- Numerical values for inputs or conversion to numerical eg female=1, male=2

(d) *Any one from:*
- Software model is more easily programmed/reprogrammed/adapted/updated hard-wired solutions must be rebuilt
- Software model is easily duplicated for testing/training/distribution each hard-wired unit must be built
- Any other valid comparison showing advantage of software model

20. (a) (i) • Image acquisition
- Capturing the (digitised) image

   (ii) *Any one from:*
- Overlapping people will confuse the outlines making outlines (of individual swimmers) difficult to detect
- Shadows being cast/reflections which will create false edges
- Waves/ripples/distortions in the water will distort the outlines making false edges
- Any valid problem with explanation

(b) 16 bits or 2 bytes

21. (a) • X=atlas_bear
- X=eastern_elk

(b) earlier(A twentieth)

(c) • Match at 11, Y is instantiated to sea_cow, <u>subgoal is extinct(X, A)</u>
- Match at 1, X is instantiated to dodo and A instantiated to seventeenth, <u>second sub-goal extinct(sea_cow,B)</u>
- Match at 2, B instantiated to eighteenth, <u>subgoal earlier(seventeenth, eighteenth)</u>
- Match at 9, <u>subgoal older(seventeenth,eighteenth)</u>
- Match at 6, all subgoals met, <u>output X=dodo</u>

(d) Flips/toggles/reverses output (from true to false or vice versa)

(e) (i)

   (ii) • Relationships are identified (using arrowed lines)
- Objects are represented by nodes

(f) *Any one from:*
- In-built searching/pattern matching/inference engine
- Goal directed searches using queries
- Use of recursion
- No algorithm to be programmed
- Any other acceptable

22. (a) DPXLFSTEC

(b) (i) *Any one from:*
- Uses less memory/memory efficient (as it only stores the current path)
- May find 'lucky' solution on left branch

   (ii) The first solution it finds is always the optimal/best solution/shortest path

(c) (i) Depth-first

    (ii) • When a node has no further descendents (X, F, S, T, etc) it is abandoned (removed from memory)
   • The search goes back to the previous node evaluated to identify another possible descendant

(d) • Calculates/evaluates all the descendant nodes/possible next moves (from node D)
   • Selects the most promising (using an evaluation function/score)
   • Moves to that node/makes that move and repeats the process until goal is found

SECTION III

Part B – Computing Networking

23. (a) The domain name server will:
   • Look up Domain Name/URL/Web Address in its database/file/list
   • Perform domain name resolution/find its <u>IP address</u>/translate URL into <u>IP address</u>
   • Return IP address to user's machine/browser or route connection for communication

  (b) *Any one from:*
   • Denial of service attack – jamming the website with bogus queries **or** bandwidth consumption/resource starvation
   • Phishing – criminals setting up a clone of the site to gather card details
   • Any other valid responses with description

  (c) Class C
   And any one from:
   • No more than 254 addresses can be assigned (the hotel does not need this many)
   • Class C would waste fewer IP addresses
   • Other classes have too many IP addresses

  (d) (i) *Any one from:*
   • Websites/URLs that are not allowed to be accessed are listed in the software
   • Websites containing keywords can be blocked

    (ii) • Selected websites/URLs are approved and listed in the software
   • Only websites on the approved list can be viewed

  (e) *Any two from:*
   • Checking Internet history
   • Intercept communications/e-mail/Internet phone
   • Access decryption keys/encrypted data

  (f) Spider – travels from one link to another on the web, gathering indexing information

   Meta-search – transmits/passes queries to several other search engines and their databases are searched and details summarised

  (g) *Any two from:*
   • Cannot format the title tag
   • No close of head
   • Closing </html> is missing its "l"

  (h) • A <u>meta tag</u> should be included (in the head section)
   • Relevant keywords added to (meta) tag
   • Any other valid

  (i) *Any one from:*
   • File virus – Attaches to the code of a program. It is run when the program is executed
   • Boot Sector Virus – Infects startup files/boot files of the OS and is executed at startup time

• Macro Virus – A virus is a macro attached to a document and runs when the document is opened (It often copies itself to the macro library as a step towards copying itself to other files)

24. (a) (i) • Node checks to see if data transfer is taking place
   • If no transfer is taking place, data is transmitted
   • If two nodes attempt to transmit at same time **or** if a collision is detected
   • Each node waits a random amount of time before attempting to re-transmit

    (ii) Time is taken to (*any one from*):
   • Check if line is free
   • Wait a random amount of time (before re-transmitting if there was a collision)
   • Increased time/traffic due to re-transmitting data

  (b) *Any combination from:*
   • Packet switching allows the network hardware to decide on the most efficient/least congested/fastest/cheapest route to take
   • Circuit switching establishes a line and uses this throughout
   or
   • Each packet can take a different route when the network is busy/congested
   • Circuit switching establishes one line and uses this throughout, (even if it is busy)
   or
   • Each packet can take a different route so if data is intercepted it will not be the whole file
   • With circuit switching the whole file can be intercepted

25. (a) (i) *Any one from:*
   • Synchronises the exchange of data
   • Defines how connections can be established/maintained/terminated
   • Performs name resolution functions turning text names for web pages into IP addresses
   • Manages log-on and password authentication

    (ii) Router

  (b) *Any one from:*
   • The data transfer rate is quicker as a start and stop frame is only needed for each packet with synchronous
   • whereas a start and stop bit is needed for each byte with asynchronous transmission
   or
   • It is much more efficient because it groups characters together into packets
   • rather than sending individual bytes one at a time

  (c) (200 * 8)/100 = 16 seconds

  (d) (i) <u>Wireless</u> network interface card/<u>Wireless</u> NIC

    (ii) *Any one from:*
   • A wireless NIC sends and receive signals to and from a wireless router/access point
   • Holds a MAC code/address (which identifies a computer on a network)
   • Accept functions of a network interface card, for example: Packaging data into frames, Data Conversion, Buffering, Auto-sensing

  (e) *Any two from:*
   • Slower transmission rates
   • More subject to interference
   • Range (Distance) is restricted
   • Less secure if not set up properly
   • Any other valid

(f) *Any one from:*
- Description of resource starvation
- Description of bandwidth consumption
- Taking advantage of bugs in networking software/exploit network management flaws
- Description of attacking the routers (Note: use "ping of death" is insufficient)
- Description of domain name server (DNS) attacks
- Any other valid

(g) (i) *Any one from:*
- Greater communication with other people via e-mail/social networking sites
- Access to more information via Internet (not just "Access to the Internet")
- Freedom of speech via on-line forums
- Other valid response

(ii) *Any one from:*
- Broader horizons/access to different cultures enriches own culture
- Gives greater access to formal and informal education
- Lack of (face-to-face) social skills
- Greater political awareness and socio-political mobility
- Other valid implication

26. (a) *Any one from:*
- Parity check will not pick up if two bits are flipped, a cyclic redundancy check can detect this type of error
- Even parity will not pick up a break in the signal, CRC would detect a badly formed packet
- CRC uses a <u>pre-defined calculation</u> (agreed by each device), Parity may differ between two machines (and cause problems)
- Any other valid comparison

(b) *Any two from:*
- Increased transfer time
- Calculations carried out at each end of transmission
- Extra data is sent eg checksum/parity

(c) *Any two from:*
- Use of anti-virus software
- Use a firewall
- Disk monitoring for possible malfunctions/Run regular diagnostic tests
- Any other valid <u>software</u> technique

(d) (i) *Any one benefit and drawback from:*
Benefit
- Makes a full backup of the network server
- Makes a copy of the configuration, software and files of the network server
- Any other valid

Drawback
- Must be kept up to date
- Backup causes a network overhead
- Any other valid

(ii) *Any one benefit and drawback from:*
Benefit
- Copies are always up-to-date
- Recovery time is very small because you just switch to the second disc
- Any other valid

Drawback
- Does not copy network configuration or software
- Mirror disk is in same device so vulnerable to physical threat
- Any other valid

SECTION III

Part C – Multimedia Technology

27. (a) Light focused onto array of <u>CCDs</u> (charge-coupled devices)
- Analogue signal sent (from CCDs) to ADC
- (ADC) converts analogue into digital

(b) No. of frames $= 12 \times 24 = 288$
No. of pixels $= 640 \times 480 = 307200$
File size = No. of frames $\times$ No. of pixels $\times$ bit depth
$= 288 \times 307200 \times 8$ bits
$= 707788800$ bits
$= 88473600$ bytes
$= 86400$ Kilobytes
$= 84.375$ Megabytes

(c) (i) Define/use a CLUT (Colour Look Up Table) for the animation

(ii) *Any two from:*
- The CLUT stores the (RGB) code for the colours used
- The stored colours are a reduced palette/subset of available colours
- These colours will be the colours displayed when the animation is on screen

(d) • Stores repeated patterns of data (in a dictionary)
• And stores a code to match these repeating blocks in the file

28. (a) ADC converts the analogue data into digital

(b) *Any one from:*
- WAV
- AIF/AIFF (Audio Interchange File Format)

(c) (i) Normalisation

(ii) *Any two from:*
- Average or peak volume is determined
- Relative sound levels are increased or decreased to bring all sounds within range
- Sound uses the full dynamic range available

(d) File size = Time $\times$ Sampling frequency $\times$ Depth $\times$ Channels
$= 300 \times 44100 \times 16 \times 2$ bits
$= 423360000$ bits
$= 52920000$ bytes
$= 51679.6875$ Kb
$= 50.5$ Mb

(e) *Any two from:*
- More channels allow more data to be held
- Better positioning of sound output/placing of instruments
- Other valid

(f) Notes stored using a list of attributes such as instrument, pitch, volume, duration, tempo

(g) • Can edit attributes of notes
• To sound differently on different channels/to create special effects

29. (a) *Any one from:*
- Bluetooth has a slow data transfer rate and video files are very large
- Bluetooth has a limited range so camera would have to be close to computer
- Other valid reason with explanation

(b) (i) Firewire/USB2.0/USB3.0

(ii) • Smooth display of live video requires fast data transfer

- Firewire has faster data transfer than USB 2.0
- Any other valid

(c) *Any two from:*
- Compression is done locally
- Local compression allows capturing of more/longer video
- File transfer times should be reduced due to the reduced file size
- Hardware codec is faster than a software codec
- Any other valid

30. (a) *Any two from:*
- WYSIWYG means slides/frames appear as they would in a viewer/player
- Author does not have to save authoring code and then view slides/frames in different viewers/players
- Author does not have to learn authoring code to create slides/frames
- Any other valid

(b) • Key frames are stored (one every five/ten/etc)
- <u>Each frame</u> is compressed (using lossy compression/JPEG is used)
- Only changes between key frames are stored. (The data that stays the same in successive frames is removed)

(c) *Any one from:*
- Resolution is limited (to a maximum of 320 × 240) but would be suitable for display in a small window
- Frame rate is limited (to 30fps) but is acceptable for smooth display (above 25fps)
- File size is limited (to 2GB) but these clips are short
- Any other valid

(d) (i) • Container files can hold several files of different types (as per multimedia presentation)
- Less complex download process as a single file to download
- Single file reduces the likelihood of missing/breaking links between component parts
- Any other valid reason with explanation

  (ii) Software/codec is needed on the receiving computer to recreate the 'contained' files

(e) *Any two from:*
- To allow hardware decoding of video/graphics files (using DSP)
- More (V)RAM to buffer data (using GPU)
- Provides additional dedicated processor
- Any other valid

31. (a) *Any two from:*
- Smaller file size/memory/backing storage (for simple/uncomplicated graphics)
- Resolution independent
- Allows editing of component objects
- Object layers can be rearranged

(b) *Any two from:*
- Texture
- Depth/Z-co-ordinate
- Direction
- Lighting

(c) *Any one from:*
- VRML (Virtual Reality Modelling Language/Virtual Reality Markup Language)
- WRL

COMPUTING HIGHER 2011

SECTION I

1. 1023 **or** $2^{10} - 1$

2. *Any one from:*
- Clock speed the number of clock cycles per second
- MIPS the number of millions of instructions per second
- FLOPS the number of floating point operations per second
- Application based tests assess computer performance in doing a series of real-world tasks

3. (a) *Any one from:*
- Buffering uses RAM Spooling uses hard disk
- Buffering is used after data is received. Spooling is used before sending data

(b) *Any two from:*
- data format conversion
- voltage conversion
- protocol conversion
- handling of status signals

4. (a) Boot sector virus

(b) • Watching
- Delivery

5. *Any one from:*
- Faster processors/clock speed
- Parallel/multi-core processors
- Larger main memory capacity
- Larger backing storage
- Faster data transfer rates/bandwidth
- Wireless technology
- NICs built into motherboards
- Any other valid

6. (a) *Any one from:*
- Vector graphic with many stored objects; file size of a bitmap does not increase as objects are added
- Vector graphic may store data on shapes hidden behind others; bitmap is single layer & does not store other data
- File size of a vector graphic increases as number of objects increases; whereas a bitmap always stays the same size

(b) (i) 2^{24} **or** 16777216 colours
  (ii) File size will increase

7. (a) Software/problem/program specification

(b) *Any one from:*
- Problem not fully specified at the first meeting with the client
- Further refinement/modification/clarification of the problem may be necessary
- Client disagreement with details given in specification

8. (a) *Any one from:*
- To identify the data/variables used at each step of the design
- To show what data is passed to/from/in/out of procedures
- To supply data to subprograms
- Identify which variables will be passed as parameters
- Identify mechanism of parameter passing (IN, OUT, IN/OUT)
- Other valid

(b) *Any two from:*
- Easy to understand/it uses English words
- Easy to convert into program code/line by line translation
- Structure of pseudocode reflects structure of modular code
- (Numbered) steps to show order/logic
- Indentation to emphasise command structures
- Pseudocode is not language specific
- Other valid

9. Stores value true/false, 1/0

10. (a) *Any one from:*
- Sections/subprograms are easily identified/implemented/tested/de-bugged/edited
- Sections/subprograms increase readability
- Independent subprograms can be added or removed easily
- Any other valid response

(b) *Any one from:*
- Internal Commentary
- Meaningful variable names
- Effective use of white space/indentation/blank lines
- Other valid

(c) *Any one from:*
- A function can only return a single value. A procedure can return any number of values
- The value of a function can be assigned to a variable. A procedure has no value

11. (a) Concatenation

(b) String

12. (a) Scripting language

(b) *Any two from:*
- Can create operations that are not readily available within the menus of the application/increase functionality
- A novice user can more easily perform complex actions
- Complex actions can be triggered by simple combination of key presses, making it easier to perform
- Access to low level operations (not available in menus)
- Adapt/alter user interface
- Same sequence of actions carried out each time the macro is run
- Other valid

SECTION II

13. (a) *Any two from:*
- Cache memory is more expensive (per megabyte)
- Cache memory has faster <u>access</u>
- Cache is Static RAM (SRAM) instead of Dynamic RAM (DRAM)
- Cache is on (or immediately adjacent to) the processor

(b) (i) *Any one from:*
- 16 GB = 137438953472bits
- 2^32 = 4294967296 memory locations
- (13743895347)/(4294967296) = 32 (bits or lines)

- 2^32 * d = 16 GB
- d = 137438953472bits/4294967296
- d = 32

- 2^{32} = 4 G
- 16/4 = 4 bytes
- 4 × 8 = 32 (bits or lines)

(ii) *Any one from:*
- Cost of RAM
- Most programs do not require maximum RAM to be installed
- Multiple addresses per location/byte addressable memory

- Some addresses assigned to I/O ports (memory mapped I/O)
- Other valid

(iii) Addressable memory size <u>doubles/increased to 32 Gb</u>

(c) • Address bus carries/holds/transfers memory address
- Data bus carries/holds/transfers data from memory location/to the processor
- Read line is activated/flagged

(d) (i) *Any one from:*
- Type of systems software that carries out a housekeeping/maintenance/support task
- Systems software which is not part of the main operating system
- Other valid

(ii) *Any two from:*
- Parts of file/unused blocks are spread across disk surface
- Each separate block/part of file requires a separate disk access
- Slows down the loading/writing of files/multiple disk access for single file

(e) *Any one from:*
- Checksum
- Heuristic detection
- (Use of) virus signatures
- Memory resident monitoring

14. (a) (i) • A client server network allows for centralised backup as all data stored on the server
- Peer-to-peer stored files across all machines so each machine has to be backed up

(ii) *Any one from:*
- No additional server/network operating system cost as peer-to-peer does not need a server/network OS
- Easy to extend as they only need to connect further machines to switch/hub etc
- Less technical knowledge required as they do not have to configure clients/server
- Security not an issue due to closed environment
- Other valid reason with suitable explanation

(b) (i)

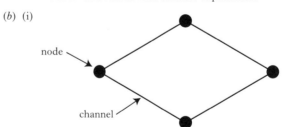

(ii) *Any one from:*
Star
- as whole network does not fail due to single channel failure
- is easier to extend by adding another branch
- any other valid
Bus
- simpler/easier to set up as it is a single wire
- easy to extend, as devices just connect to spine
- any other valid

(c) (i) *Any two from:*
- Print resolution/dpi
- Number of colours/colour depth/black & white/grey scale
- Print speed/ppm
- Buffer capacity/amount of RAM
- Type of interface/data transfer speed/serial to parallel
- Operating System/Driver

(ii) *Any one from:*
- Manage processes/Resource allocation ensures processor time and memory are allocated to the process
- Input output management sends and receives signals from the printer
- Memory management allocates memory and locates data in memory to be sent to printer
- Interpret user commands (CLI) receives user commands to print data
- File Management will locate and retrieve the file from backing storage
- Error reporting will report any problems with the printer, eg Printer out of paper etc.

(d) *Any one from:*
- Provides a queuing facility for print jobs
- May maximise efficiency of printer use by distributing jobs
- Stores (multiple) print jobs/jobs from (multiple) computers
- Organises/prioritises printing queue
- Other valid

(e) *Any two from:*
- Solid state storage is more robust than mechanical hard drive
- Capacities of solid state storage are increasing
- Decreasing price of solid state
- SSD has faster access times
- On board encryption facility
- Lower power requirements
- Any other valid

15. (a) *Any two from:*
- Code is attached to on-screen events eg buttons/Events trigger the code
- Predefined routines for the creation of buttons/form/GUIs etc
- Flow of control is determined by user actions

(b) (i) Procedural
   (ii) *Any one from:*
   - Use of subprograms, one for each service on offer
   - Program control using sequence – to go through initial identification procedure, and selection – to carry out chosen service
   - Range of data types are available

(c) Total=0
   For each option() chosen that day
   If option(current) = mobile top-up then
     add 1 to total
   end if
   next transaction

(d) *Any two from:*
- Testing is planned in advance/creation of a test plan
- which includes test data to be used and the expected results
- will be followed in a logical order
- Involves testing of subprograms/subroutines/ components/modules/programs individually and together

(e) *Any one from:*
- Testing is as thorough as possible
- Covers a wide/full range of possibilities
- Data should in range, out of range and boundary data

(f) *Any one from:*
- Compiled version of code can be saved, no need for translation every time program is run
- Will not be translated each time program is run, more processor efficient

- Translator software not required, more memory efficient
- Compiled version is saved   details of code are protected from theft/alteration/copying
- Any other valid point   explanation of consequence

(g) Perfective
A new feature is being added that was not originally required

16. (a) (i) *Any one from:*
   - Software performs as predicted on duplicated test runs
   - Software will not stop due to design flaws
   - Output is correct for all specified inputs
   (ii) *Any one from:*
   - No unnecessary code is included in the program, processor not required to carry out unnecessary commands
   - Minimise the number of disk accesses/peripherals, reducing time processor will have to stand idle
   - Simple user interface as complex interfaces take some time to draw etc
   - Use of Nested IFs/Case statements to logically structure code to avoid testing unnecessary conditions
   - Valid programming example explanation of processor efficiency

(b) (i) *Any one from:*
   - Current value (of variable) passed into a subprogram for use
   - To allow data to be passed by value
   - Protect (original value of) variable from change by subprogram
   (ii) *Any one from:*
   - Data/variables (created within procedure and only) passed out of a subprogram
   - Brand new variable is passed out of subprogram

(c) *Any one from:*
- Programmers will each be writing individual subprograms for the software required, reducing implementation time **or** so they must collaborate via meetings/project manager/detailed plan
- Will discuss how to implement the design/get help from more experienced programmer/discuss testing to reduce time wasted/find and solve problems earlier/ensure testing is systematic and comprehensive
- Any other valid technique/topic and description

(d) *Any one from:*
- Can carry out a complex operation that they could not write themselves
- Do not have to design the solution to the subproblem

(e) (i) *Any two from:*
   - a list of data/(fixed) number of items
   - items are the same data type/array has a single data type
   - position of data identified by its position/index/ element/subscript
   (ii) *Any one from:*
   - Parameter passing list will use one array rather than a list of variables
   - Do not need to write a line of code to manipulate each data item individually, operation can be performed on each item in the array using a loop

(f) *Any one from:*
Pascal: =word[5]+word[6]+word[7] **or**
           =concat(word[5],word[6],word[7])
Java: =word.substring(4,7)
Visual Basic: = right(word,3) **or** =mid(word,5,3)
TrueBasic: = word$(5:7)

SECTION III

Part A – Artificial Intelligence

17. (*a*) (i) *Any one from:*

Problem solving, memory, learning, creativity, cognitive ability, other valid

(ii) *Any one from:*

- Uses natural language which is a high order skill
- Uses a greater variety of human intelligence skills rather than manipulate a closed world of chess rules
- Requires the integration of human intelligence (in the same way that people do) instead of following of best path
- Uses judgement to decide levels of confidence for response
- Larger domain of knowledge required in quiz game, Chess has a much narrower simplistic domain
- Any other valid with justification in context

(*b*) (i) *Any two from:*

- Natural Language Understanding NLU – checking it is a valid sentence, extracting meaning for the sentence/phrase, resolve ambiguity
- Natural Language Generation NLG – formulating a suitable response to the sentence/question
- Speech Synthesis – outputting the response in the form of sound/voice

(ii) *Any one from:*

- "ship of the desert" is a metaphor/ambiguous which could prove difficult because its literal sense is impossible
- question/answer on 'surfing' is an example of changing nature of language, ambiguity used within the question/answer

(*c*) *Any one from:*

Faster processors would execute searches of knowledge in less time.

Parallel processing:
- would enable multiple responses to be evaluated simultaneously
- to search possible responses to select the one to use

Cache
- would shorten the time for fetching and executing instructions to arrive at a response more quickly.

18. (*a*) (i) *Any one from:*

- Inference engine – performs pattern matching/searching on the rules using information gathered
- User interface – gathers information from the user by presenting options/choices and provides output to user

(ii) *Any one from:*

- Asking the user questions (to add responses)
- By selecting/applying rules (and adding the conclusion)

(*b*) (i) *Any one from:*

- Determines if the software is fit for purpose by meeting the software specification
- Determines if the software is correct by giving the correct output for the specified input
- Determines if the software is robust by handling invalid input

(ii) *Any one from:*

- Only the lawyers have the knowledge to know if the output is correct
- Only the lawyers will understand the terminology of the output documents
- Any other reasonable response

(*c*) Internet makes it available to users worldwide but laws vary from country to country or region to region

(*d*) *Any one from:*

- Laws can change requiring maintenance
- Novel situations for which there are no applicable rules
- No common sense so limited to application of existing facts/rules
- Expert system may be out of date Lawyer has more up-to-date knowledge
- Any other reasonable situation with description

(*e*) *Any one from:*

Dendral	identifying unknown organic molecules
Mycin	identify bacteria causing severe infections
Rice-Crop Doctor	diagnoses pests and diseases for rice crops
AGREX/CALEX	areas of fertilizer application, crop protection, irrigation scheduling, and diagnosis of diseases
Variex	advises selection of the best cultivators for different agricultural situations
Weiping Jin Expert System	advice on crop management
LEY Expert System	automated, remote, real-time weather data acquisition and reporting system
CLIPS	to reach conclusions concerning profitable alfalfa production
CaDet	decision support system for Early Cancer Detection
DXplain	Medical diagnosis
Puff	diagnoses the results of pulmonary function tests
Seth	advice concerning the treatment and monitoring of drug poisoning
PEIRS	(Pathology Expert Interpretative Reporting System) appends interpretative comments to chemical pathology reports
R1 or XCON or XSEL	automatically selecting the computer system components based on the customer's requirements.

19. (*a*) (i) ●●●○_○○ **or** bbbw_ww

(ii) *Any one from:*
- ●_●●○○○ **or** b_bbwww
- ●●○●_○○ **or** bbwb_ww

(iii) *Any two from:*
- A path ends, or is blocked, as there are no possible other moves/descendants – there are no more legal moves for the stones from this point
- The algorithm moves back to the previously stored state/move/arrangement of stones
- To evaluate another possible move/descendant – try to move a different stone

(*b*) • The first solution it finds is always the best solution.
• Won't get stuck in a loop down one branch.

(*c*) Heuristic (search)

20. (a)

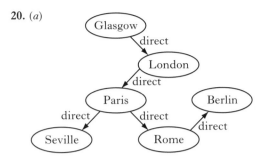

(b) Part of a rule that is satisfied for the goal to be satisfied/met

(c) X=rome, X=seville

(d) ?direct(X, rome), direct(X, seville)
?fly_direct(X rome) AND fly_direct(X seville)

(e) • Match at 7 X instantiated to glasgow, sub_goal
fly_direct(glasgow, Z)
• Match at 6 P instantiated to glasgow, sub_goal
direct(glasgow, Q)
• Match at 1 Q instantiated to london **or**
Z instantiated to london
• Second sub-goal of rule 7, fly_direct(london, Y)
• Match at 6 P instantiated to london, sub_goal
direct(london, Q)
• Match at 2 Q instantiated to paris/Y instantiated to paris.
Y=paris is output

SECTION III

Part B – Computer Networking

21. (a) A – html
B – title
C – body

(b) Project Manager

(c) (i) *Any one from:*
• Can check availability of activities instantly so if not available, you can easily check another one
• Less chance of "worker"/"human" error as you can check the final screen
• Pay before going on holiday so you don't need as much money with you on holiday/reduces queuing when on holiday
• Know in advance what activities you will be taking part in so can bring requirements with you (for example: swimming suit)
• Can book 24/7 so are not confined to normal office hours/more chance to make booking
• Can book from any location so no need to travel to location/take time out of holiday to make booking
• Any other valid benefit with appropriate reasoning

(ii) *Any one from:*
• Customers may not think of the cost as "holiday money"
• Some activities "look better" online
• Good advertising
• Customers have more time to book (24/7)
• Any other valid answer

(iii) *Any one from:*
• Use a secure protocol such as HTTPS
• Encryption
• Digital certificates
• Use a secure 3rd party payment service
• Any other valid answer

(d) • WML doesn't support many text formats
• WML has problems with tables (due to their width)
• Restricted graphic format/standard JPG/GIF/PNG Web formats cannot be displayed without conversion (to WBMP format)
• Any other valid answer

22. (a) 200 * 8 * 1024 = 1,638,400 Kilobits
1,638,400 Kilobits/512/60 = 53.3 minutes

(b) *Any two from*
• To standardise the transmission of data between computer systems on networks
• To allow different computer systems to communicate and work together on a network
• To show how different protocols work at different levels in a network OS/environment

(c) (i) • IP adds an address (header) to each packet
• IP routes the packets around the network
(ii) File Transfer Protocol/FTP

(d) *Any one from:*
• The message is divided into packets
• Each individual packet can take a different path through the network
• Packets are re-assembled at destination

(e) (i) • Double errors cancel each other out so error would not be spotted
• For example: when using even parity, 0001 001 with parity bit 0 is received as 1000 001 with parity bit 0, the parity check will not fail since the reversal of the 1st and 4th bits leaves the parity bit unchanged
or
• Where sender and receiver are using different parities
• For example: when using even parity; 0001 001 with parity bit 0 is received as 0000 001 with parity bit 0 which should indicate an error, but the receiver is using odd parity and therefore parity check would not fail
(ii) *Any one from:*
• (Time will be taken to) carry out the calculation of the parity bit
• (Time will be taken to) send the extra parity bit
• (Time will be taken to) perform the parity check

23. (a) (i) Denial of Service Attack/DOS
(ii) *Any two from:*
• Loss of business
• Cost of employing experts to analyse the attack
• Cost of placing preventative measures for future attacks
(iii) *Any two from:*
• IP address filtering/Filters out IP addresses/block selected IP addresses access to local area network
• Prevents access to network from particular ports/monitor all communication ports
• Inspects incoming packets for suspicious activity

(b) *Any two from:*
• A switch reduces network traffic due to it directing the packet/data to a specific station
• There are fewer collisions due to a switch allocating the whole bandwidth to each connected computer

(c) (i) • The first octet is between 192 and 223
• The first three octets are fixed
(ii) It is different to the original which indicates a different network
(iii) It is greater than 255/Out of range

(d) *Any two from:*
- If more than one transmission takes place there will be a collision and data will have to <u>wait a random amount of time</u>
- If more than one transmission takes place there will be a collision and data will have to be <u>re-sent</u>
- Before transmitting data time is taken to check if the line is free

24. (a) (i) • A meta-search engine transmits/passes queries to several other search engines
- and their databases are searched
- and details summarised in a list

(ii) Spiders **or** Meta-Tags

(b) SMTP is used for <u>sending/transfer/transmit</u> e-mails

(c) *Any two from:*
- Lack of face to face communication/social skills
- Health issues/lack of exercise
- Safety issues/access to inappropriate people
- Security issues/children giving out personal details
- Access to inappropriate material
- Any other appropriate answer

(d) (i) There is a list of acceptable websites
- restricted view of the Internet
- all other websites are blocked

(ii) *Any one from:*
- Number of web sites that could be viewed is too limited.
- Child can only access websites deemed suitable by the parent.

(iii) This filters out particular keywords/websites and allows access to all others.

(e) (i) Access to a broad range of information **and** the skill to use it.

(ii) *Any two from:*
Information Rich enables you to:
- Make informed decisions and choices
- Inform individual and business research/projects/tasks
- Facilitate individual educational progress
- Improve individual leisure pursuits
- Improve individual job prospects
- Any other valid answer

SECTION III

Part C – Multimedia Technology

25. (a) (i) • Scanner uses single linear CCD(s)
- Digital camera uses a CCD array/grid

(ii) Uses intermediate shades of colour in surrounding pixels

(iii) Rescan the logo using a higher resolution than the original scan.
or
Software adds extra <u>smaller</u> pixels to blend in.

(b) *Any one from:*
- Vector graphic is resolution independent and so will always be displayed to the best effect
- Logo is few objects and so vector graphic will have a small file size

26. (a) (i) Data being transferred and viewed before entire file has been received

(ii) • No permanent copy of file stored on visitor's computer
- So reduces opportunity for illegal copying

(b) • To decompress the streamed file
- To decrease transfer time

(c) *Any two from:*
- Hardware codecs use own GPU/processor rather than CPU
- Coding/decoding will consequently be quicker
- and so file can be played at correct rate

(d) *Any one from:*
Volume/Instrument/Pitch/Channel

(e) Voice or other recorded/sampled sound

(f) (i) • MIDI files are easy to manipulate
- Individual attributes can be changed

(ii) *Any one from:*
- Sound card generates sound from MIDI file depends on capability of sound card/may not be same as original recording.
- MP3 is a bit mapped/sampled sound so the original sound is not reproduced.
- Valid fact with valid explanation

(iii) • MP3 does not store sounds that humans cannot hear/emphasises sounds humans can hear best
- MP3 does not store sounds that are drowned out by louder sounds
- and then uses the Huffman compression technique.

27. (a) (i) Can plan the order of the clips/the effects to be applied.

(ii) *Any one from:*
Fade/Wipe/Dissolve/Hard cut/Peel/page turn/any other valid

(b) File size = $(4 \times 60 \times 15)$ = 3600 frames
= **3600** $\times (24 \times 720000)$ bits
= 62208000000 bits = 7776000000 bytes = 7.24 Gb

(c) • Key frames are stored (one every five/ten/etc)
- Each frame is compressed (using lossy compression/JPEG is used)
- Only changes between key frames are stored. (The data that stays the same in successive frames is removed)

(d) *Any one from:*
- Frame size/resolution is limited (to a maximum of 320 by 240) but would be suitable for display in a small window
- Frame rate is limited (to 30fps) but is acceptable for smooth display (above 25fps)

(e) • ADC converts analogue data into digital data
- DSP compresses/adds effects to digital data

28. (a) File size = $(60 \times 44100) \times 2 \times 32$ bits
= 169344000 bits = 20.2 Mb

(b) PCM (Pulse Code Modulation)

(c) (i) A container file allows the storage of a variety of data types as a single file.

(ii) *Any two from:*
- All necessary files can be distributed as single item more likely that customer will receive all that is required for lesson.
- RIFF is a common file format and accessible by different platforms.

(d) (i) Normalisation
Any one from:
- Increases or decreases the sound levels to an average value.
- Causes sound levels to use the full dynamic range available.

(ii) Clipping

(iii) *Any one from:*
- Volume edited to beyond the dynamic range
- A special effect may have been added.

(e) (i) • DVDs have data on 1 or 2 sides of the disc
- Holographic discs have the data stored through the thickness of the disc/in more than 2 layers

(ii) • Holographic discs can be read in parallel
- Whereas DVDs are read one layer at a time

COMPUTING HIGHER 2012

SECTION I

1. 585

2. (a) Exponent

   (b) Mantissa

3. *Any two from:*
- Each pixel represented as a binary number
- As a (2D) array/grid of pixels
- Colour (of pixel) represented by (unique) binary value/notion of bit depth

4. *Any two from:*
- Voltage conversion
- Data format conversion/serial to parallel/analogue to digital
- Handling of status signals (accept a valid example)

5. • 1) Registers
   • 3) RAM/ROM/Main Memory

6. (a) *Any two from:*
- Decide where on backing store the file will be saved
- Allocate/record address of file
- Ensure that file does not overwrite existing/valid data
- Define access rights
- Record the creation date
- Update the file directory
- Any other valid

   (b) *Any one from:*
- Copies/transfers the blocks of data from main memory to the hard disk
- Handles errors during data transfer
- Inputting user commands for save via mouse click etc.
- Any other valid

7. (a) Bus

   (b) *Any one from:*
- Better security/control of access
- Efficient backup of centralised files
- File/application sharing is simpler to set up
- Any other valid

   (c) *Any one from:*
- A router
- A (cable) modem
- Any other valid

8. • The process may revisit an earlier stage
   • In the light of experience/information gained

9. A problem is broken down into smaller/easier to solve (sub-)problems.

10. *Any one from:*
- Structure chart/diagram
- Flowchart
- Semantic net
- Any other valid

11. (a) *Any one from:*
- Implementation
- Testing
- Maintenance

    (b) Implementation: lines of code are translated and executed in turn, reporting syntax errors
    Testing: test all (or part) of code to help identify line where error occurs
    Maintenance: as above

12. *Any one from:*
- Scripting language is embedded within an application whereas a procedural is stand-alone
- Keywords within a scripting language are specific to parent application whereas in a procedural keywords are more general
- Programmer has control over data types/might have access to low level commands/operations in a procedural language whereas data types are embedded in a scripting language

13. (*a*) A variable which can have only 2 values – true/false

(*b*) *Any one from:*
- Used to terminate the loop
- Used to show the presence of the item in the list

14. Reliable software:
Any one from:
- Will give correct output to valid data
- Will not stop due to design flaws/errors
- Free from design and coding bugs
Robust software will not crash when invalid data is entered

15. *Any one from:*
- Will detail test data originally used so that re-testing on that data will not need to be done again
- Details the original test data which did not find the error
- Allows identification of new data sets that should be tested

16. *Any two from:*
- Use of meaningful variable names
- Use of internal comments
- Effective use of white space
- Use of procedures/modularity/subroutines/functions
- Use of parameter passing/local variables
- Use of module libraries
- Use of formatted keywords
- Any other valid

SECTION II

17. (*a*) *Any one from:*
- Clock speed does not take other important architectural features into consideration (such as data bus width)
- Clock speed is not a measure of actual throughput.
- Clock speed is only valid if the processors being compared have the same architecture.

(*b*) *Any two from:*
- FLOPS result may be more reliable as (logic/arithmetic) operations independent of level of complexity
- Complexity of instructions used can vary (and therefore skew the results with MIPS)
- MIPS test may have been performed with small/simple machine instructions

(*c*) Addressable memory = 2^{32} x 128
= 549755813888 bits =68719476736 bytes
= 67108864 Kbytes = 65536 Mbytes = 64Gbytes.

(*d*) (i) AND, OR, NOT, =, <, <=, >, >=, <>, etc.

(ii) *Any one from:*
- Synchronise processor instructions/operations
- Control the flow of data/instructions within CPU
- Activate and/or respond to control lines
- Control fetch execute cycle
- Decode and execute instructions.

(*e*) More data can be carried in a single instruction cycle/at one time

18 (*a*) *Any two from:*
- Each computer on a network has its own built in processor/RAM/backing storage
- A terminal is reliant on the processor/RAM/backing storage capacity of the mainframe
- A mainframe will have many thousands of processors / massive ram space/ backing storage
- Much more than any individual computer on a computer network

(*b*) (i) • The available free space is fragmented, file fragments/space spread out over the disks
- Large section of (contiguous) free space required to store the file
or
- Disk contains unidentified bad sectors
- These are unavailable for storing of data
or
- Disk space used by copies of virus that does not show in file table
- But these blocks are unavailable for storing data

(ii) A defragmenter
or
disk editor
or
anti-virus

(iii) Utility software

(*c*) Copper/UTP/fibre optic/co-axial/wireless/WiFi
Any valid reason (range/bandwidth/security) that allows at least 80 metres range with large files

(*d*) Address (of the data to be read) placed on the address bus (by the processor)
The read line is set high/activated
Data (from the memory location) transferred (to the processor) using the data bus

19. (*a*) Unicode
Unicode can represent all 3000 chars, ASCII can only represent up to 256/8 bit

(*b*) *Any two from:*
- DPI/Resolution
- Compatibility/interface
- Buffer capacity
- Printing speed/PPM
- Physical size/portable

(*c*) (i) A file virus cannot infect a data file only an executable file

(ii) A virus is (self-)replicating code

(iii) *Any one from:*
- Camouflage
- Watching
- Delivery
- Replication

(*d*) *Any two from:*
- 8 bit colour/8 bits per pixel/256 colours
- Bitmapped format
- Transparency
- (Lossless) compression {but not lossy compression}
- Supports simple animation
- Standard file format (high level of compatibility)

SECTION II

20. (a) (i) *Any one from:*
- (Interview client management) to establish <u>precisely</u> what is needed elicit details
- (Interview current users of the system) to establish good/bad points of current system
- Any other valid explanation

(ii) *Any two from:*
- Issue questionnaires
- Make observation notes/observe current practice
- Examine sources of information/company documentation

(b) (i) Software specification/program specification/ORD

(ii) *Any two from:*
- Formalises the <u>details</u> of the software to be produced
- It will form part of a legal agreement/contract
- If one of client s needs is omitted from the document, it will not be done as part of the initial contract
- Additional features cannot be added into software without new contract
- Any other valid reason

(c) *Any one from:*
- Contribute to the provision of test data
- Plan structure of testing to match boundaries/analysis
- Validate test data to be used at testing stage
- Validate test results against specification
- Any other valid

(d) Since he has involvement with the project he doesn t qualify

(e) Systematic
- Tests individual subroutines, then modules, up to whole system testing
- Methodical/logical/planned checking of software

Comprehensive
- Uses normal/extreme/exceptional data
- Test software in as many cases as possible/full range

(f) Project manager

21. (a) (1-D) Array of real

(b) tallest = height[1]
name_of_winner = name[1]
loop to end of list
    if height[position]>tallest then
        tallest = height[position]
        name_of_winner = name[position]
    end if
end loop
display name_of_winner (1 mark)
or
max = 1
for position = 1 to end of list do
    if height[position]> height[max] then
        max = position
    end if
end loop
display name[max]

(c) (i) *Any one from:*
- Change initial condition to smallest = height[1]
- Change > to < OR 'change greater than to less than'
- Change variable names to eg tallest to smallest / max to min
- Change output line

(ii) *Any one from:*
- Change initial condition to smallest = height[1] which can be reset when a lower value is found
- Change > to < since looking for smaller values than the current one
- Change variable names to eg tallest to smallest/max to min to reflect meaningful variable names
- Change output line to reflect change in variable name/new context if name is in descriptive text

22. (a) The first IF is true, but the second and third IFs will still be evaluated wasting processor time

(b) <u>Nested IF</u>
IF cost per person is less than 500
    set band to 'cheap'
ELSE IF (cost per person less than 2000)
    set band to 'medium';
ELSE
    Set band to 'expensive';
(END IF)

or … <u>CASE statement</u>
CASE cost per person OF
    IS < 500 : set band to 'cheap';
    IS < 2000 : set band to 'medium';
Otherwise
    Set band to 'expensive'
(END CASE)

(c) By value since the value is not being changed in the procedure

(d) Joining/adding together of (sub-)strings

(e) A (self-contained/discrete/named) module/unit/block/section of code which has a value/ returns a single value to the calling program

SECTION III PART A: ARTIFICIAL INTELLIGENCE

23. (a) Test a system/device/program for presence of (artificial) intelligence

(b) *Any two from:*
- Identifies keywords/phrases from human sentence
- Matches an appropriate response (from bank)
- If there isn t a match, makes a generic response or another start point

(c) *Any two from:*
- May fail to store previous responses
- Inability to include current or topical statements
- Inability to problem solve in conversation
- Inability to comprehend humour/emotion
- Vocabulary/grammar may be artificial/unusual
- Any other valid

(d) Any one of increased clock speed/presence of cache/increased cache/multiple processors

Any valid description of how performance is improved ie
- Multiple threads/queries improving searching/pattern matching
- Faster execution producing faster responses

24. (a) Problem solving

(b) The computer is merely following instructions of the (intelligent) programmer/human.

(c) Search tree

(d) Breadth-first (1) because
- All possible descendants from the start state have been generated
- Node(0,5) would not be generated yet in depth-first
- Node(3,5) would have been discarded in depth-first

(e) Depth-first and Heuristic

(f) (0,3)

(g) *Any two from:*
- Empty 3 litre jug
- Empty 5 litre jug
- Fill the 3 litre jug from the 5 litre jug/Pour the 5 litre jug into the 3 litre jug

25. (a) *Any two from:*
- Flat/ two-dimensional viewpoint, eliminating/reducing problems with 3D depth perception
- Light variation/shadows have been reduced/eliminated by the use of a lamp
- Edge detection of rectangular objects with straight lines is simpler.
- Tiles on known background colour/conveyor belt

(b) 32 bit colour= 4294967296 (accept 2^{32})

(c) *Any two from:*
- Signal processing convert signal into form that can be understood/ digitisation /"clean up" signal
- Edge detection identify sharp changes in colour/tone/ light as edges, making a wireframe model
- Object recognition wireframe model is matched against templates of known objects
- Image understanding analysis of collection of objects give sense of whole image

(d) *Any three from:*
- Weights will be initially set
- Known inputs will be used and outputs compared to expected
- Weights altered/rebalanced to achieve the known output
- Process repeated until all inputs and outputs match

(e) *Any one from:*
- Vision system for lane control in a car.
- Vision system used to inform sat nav
- Any other valid vision system <u>embedded</u> in a larger system

26. (a) *Any one from:*
- Machines/computers/programs capable of doing task that would require intelligence if done by human
- Ability of system to display/emulate intelligent human behaviour
- Any other valid

(b) *Any one from:*
- Ability to make decisions independent of external control
- The ability to learn/problem solve/etc
- Any other valid

(c) *Any two from:*
- Power supply - battery needs recharging, attaching power cable hinders mobility
- Vision system - detecting and avoiding obstacles/stairs
- Navigation - planning a path or limiting the path using virtual walls across doorways
- Type of terrain - choosing tools for cleaning different surfaces
Note: the marks could come from the same bullet

(d) (i) Where responsibility lies in the event of an accident (or other valid)

(ii) *Any one from:*
- Use a disclaimer (denying responsibility for accidents caused by not following instructions.)
- Any method of avoiding accidents such as audible signals etc.
- Any other valid

27. (a) X=druid

(b) ? is_weapon_against(X troll)

(c)
- life_points(troll, 800) would be false/no.
- not(life_points(troll, 800)) would be true

(d)
- Match at 13 X instantiated to troll, <u>subgoal has_found(troll Z)</u>
- Match at 1 Z instantiated to jewel, <u>subgoal is_weapon_against(jewel Y)</u>
- Match at 8, Y=troll, new <u>subgoal troll=troll is true</u>
- <u>not(troll=troll) is false,</u> subgoal fails
- Backtrack to match at 2, Z instantiated to sword, new subgoal <u>is_weapon_against(sword, Y)</u>
- Match at 7, Y=orc <u>not(troll=orc) succeeds</u>
- <u>Output Y=orc</u>

(e) (i) stronger_than(X Y)

(ii) Corrective

SECTION III PART B: COMPUTER NETWORKING

28. (a) (i) Network

(ii) Presentation

(b)
- IP adds its own header/address header/source/ destination/IP header to each packet.
- IP routes the packets around the network.

(c)
- It reduces the number of collisions on a network therefore reducing the amount of data that would have to be re-transmitted
or
- It reduces simultaneous transmissions therefore reducing collisions

(d) Odd Parity
Any one justification from:
- there is an odd number of ones/zeros
- five ones to be transmitted
- there was an even number of ones before the parity bit was added

(e) Asynchronous
Any one from:
- Asynchronous uses start and stop bits around each byte/character/word
- Synchronous uses a start and stop **frame** for each **packet** of data. It does **not** use a start/stop bit.

29. (a) *Any one from:*
- Security - computers must be physically connected to access the network/<u>harder</u> to intercept data
- <u>Less</u> interference/signal drop-off
- Bandwidth - Faster transmission speeds

(b) Passive Attack

(c) <title> White Tooth </title>

(d) *Any one from:*
- 16,777,216 colours
- 16.7 million colour
- 2^{24} colours
- 24 bit colour

(e) (i) Metatag (with keywords)

(ii) Header/head

(f) (i) Wireless Markup Language/WML

(ii) WAP

(iii) PDA/palmtop/Pager/2-way Radio/Any other valid

(g) Corrective

30. (*a*) Telnet

(*b*) (i) *Any one from:*
- Bandwidth consumption - This degrades the server performance by sending a large number of data packets in a short period of time.
- Resource starvation - An attack which is intended to use resources that would bring the network down. For example, an e-mail inbox could be bombarded with e-mails and so would fill up and therefore not allow genuine e-mails through.
- Programming flaws - This takes advantage of bugs in networking software.
- Attacking the routers - This involves "hi-jacking" data packets and routing them to the target server, which then gets flooded with data packets, or re-directing them to false addresses.
- Domain Name Server attacks/IP Spoofing - This involves sending a large number of DNS queries with a spoofed IP address of the target server. The DNS then floods the target server with an excessive amount of replies.

(ii) *Any two from:*
- Cost of determining the nature of the attack
- Cost of repair and response to the attack
- Cost of devising and implementing safeguards
- Cost of additional admin to compensate for loss of network services
- Any other valid cost

(*c*) *Any two from:*
- Monitors all communication ports/checks packets/block ports
- Keeps track of all communications/makes user log
- Blocks unauthorised access/prevents unsolicited traffic
- IP Filtering

(*d*) *Any two from:*
- Authenticate the user – a "callback" facility to correct phone line/IP address
- Set user permissions allocating the minimum necessary access to each user/levels of access
- Encrypting data to make data unreadable/give each employee a restricted key
- Use a secure protocol such as HTTPS to make data unreadable in transit
- Other valid method showing how it prevents access

(*e*) *Any two from:*
- It creates a backup
- Which allows data to be saved to several disks at the same time
- Creates an exact /up-to-date copy of the data on the server

(*f*) (i) • List of approved website/URLs (in the software)
- Only approved websites can be viewed/all others are blocked

(ii) *Any one from:*
- Unsuitable websites/URLs are listed in the Internet Filtering software
- Websites containing certain keywords/content/file types/domain names can be blocked

(*g*) *Any one from:*
- Uses wireless transmission/no cables
- Across a very short range
- Low power consumption
- Any other valid

31. (*a*) *Any one from:*
- Class A allows 16,777,214 addresses (2^{24}- 2)
- A small network would use class C (with 254 addresses)
- Only 12 IP addresses are needed

(*b*) (Uniquely) identifies a computer/device (on a network).

(*c*) *Any three from:*
- The original/same calculation is carried out
- A comparison is made to the original
- If there is a difference, there has been an error/data will need to be retransmitted
- If the results match the data will be accepted

(*d*) (i) • (Splits the data into small parts and) each packet may take a different route to its destination
- Unlikely to intercept all packets/the whole file

(ii) Circuit switching

(*e*) (i) • (150 * 8) = 1,200 Megabits
- 1,200 / 8 = 150 seconds (/ 60 = 2.5 minutes)
or
- 8 megabits per second = 1 megabyte per second
- 150 megabytes takes 150 seconds (/ 60 = 2.5 minutes)

(ii) *Any two from:*
- Bad packets needing re-sent/collisions of data
- Rest of message frame (parity etc) takes up space and hence bandwidth
- Another part of the network may have a slower connection
- Sharing bandwidth with other users/processes
- Integrity checks on file
- Any other valid

SECTION III PART C: MULTIMEDIA TECHNOLOGY

32. (*a*) (i) *Any two from:*
- Can be replayed on any musical instrument with a MIDI interface (eg keyboard, synthesiser, drum machine)
- Accuracy of playback sound not necessary for practise
- Individual instruments/notes can be edited or have effects added
- Backing tracks unlikely to include voice
- No interference/white noise/background sounds

(ii) Duration – length (number of beats) of a <u>note</u> Tempo – speed at which music is to be replayed/ number of beats per minute (bpm)

(*b*) *Any two from:*
- MP3 can be played on a wider variety of players than MIDI
- MP3 produces a more natural sound
- MIDI sound can vary as same "instrument" may differ between devices
- Any other valid

(*c*) No. of frames = 64 × 25 = 1600
No. of pixels = 1024 × 768 = 786432

File size = No. of frames × No. of pixels x bit depth
= <u>1600 x 786432</u> × <u>24 bits</u>
= 30198988800 bits = 3774873600 bytes = 3686400 Kb
= 3600 Mb

(*d*) No permanent copy on pupil computer

(*e*) • If data buffered is viewed before next block is stored/received
- Then video is paused until next block is stored/received

33. (a) *Any two from:*
- Faster data transfer rate (up to 4.8 Gbits per sec)
- USB interface more common on current computer hardware
- USB3.0 has backward compatibility with previous USB interfaces
- Any other valid

(b) *Any one from:*
- Wireless connectivity already available (even if limited)
- WiFi reduces battery life
- Extra weight/ larger device
- Any other valid

(c) No moving parts/motor so less power is required

(d) Advantage: faster compression/processing rate
Disadvantage: cannot be (easily) upgraded

(e) (i) Allows an effect to be used when clips are joined together

(ii) *Any one from:*
- Wipe – line moves across first clip replacing it with next clip
- Fade out/in – clip gradually dwindles to black/ emerges from black
- Dissolve – first clip gradually morphs into next clip
- Hard cut – first clip changes instantly to next clip
- Page turn – first clip peels away from screen to show next clip
- Other valid answer – with description

(f) EasyVid3 and EasyVid4 data is already captured/stored in digital

34. (a) *Any two from:*
- Shows timing/transitions between screens
- Gives content of screens eg placement of items/layout, actual content, backgrounds, colour schemes
- Gives navigation links/hyperlinks
- Any other valid

(b) File size = $11000 \times 24 \times 8 \times 2$ bits
= 4224000 bits = 528000 bytes = 515.625 Kb
= 515.6 Kb

(c) (i) ADPCM (Adaptive Delta Pulse Code Modulation/ Adaptive Differential Pulse Code Modulation)

(ii)
- Stores a sampled sound then change between sound samples (not the actual samples)
- Compression is because number of bits required to store change between samples is less than sample amplitude value.

(d) Storing recordings in mono would half storage required
or
Edit out pauses et cetera to shorten the clip

(e) Fade in

(f) (i) Graph must show flat (clipped) section(s)
Clipping occurs when sound outwith the dynamic range is lost

(ii)
- It calculates average volume/level
- Scales amplitudes/volumes to bring everything within dynamic range

(iii)
- Every sound in the file is affected therefore background noise will also be boosted

35. (a)
- Vector graphic formats store each object (and its attributes) separately
- Adding another object requires more data to be stored (so file size increases)

(b) *Any two from:*
- Vector graphic formats are displayed at hardware's resolution/resolution independent
- So scaling will not affect image quality in vector
- Bitmaps become pixelated if graphic is scaled up

(c) It will be a lighter /paler shade of green

(d) (i) *Any one from:*
- Dithering uses patterns of existing colours to create illusion of additional colours (not in palette/at bit depth)
- Two (or more) adjacent coloured pixels create the illusion of another colour (not in the palette)

(ii)
- PNG allows 2^{24} (16 million) colours
- More colours are not required/this is true colour

(e) (i) To smooth jagged edges of curves/diagonals

(ii) *Any one from:*
- Image scanned/drawn/displayed at low resolution
- Improve the look of a (low resolution/pixelated) image
- Description of other valid situation

COMPUTING HIGHER 2013

SECTION I

1. Advantage: Unicode allows larger range of characters/character set/more alphabets to be represented

   Disadvantage: Unicode requires larger memory/backing store size (as it uses 16 bits per char)

2. 24(bits)

3. *Any two from:*
   - (Image is stored as a) grid of pixels/2D Array of pixels
   - Number of bits represents the range of colours/bit depth
   - (unique) binary number for each colour
   - each pixel represented as a binary number/byte/bit

4. (*a*) Macro virus

   (*b*) *Any one from:*
   - Anti-virus software not kept up to date/new virus not detected by anti-virus software
   - Anti-virus software may have been switched off/developed a fault
   - Virus is camouflaged/dummy lines of code added to virus/lines of virus code appear in different order/polymorphic virus

5. *Any one of following:*
   - Data can be saved to fast backing storage/HD/etc
   - sent to the printer as and when it is ready/RAM free to receive it

6. Reset/Interrupt/NMI/Clock/other valid

7. Diagram A: The network cannot operate
   Diagram B: No effect on the network/Nodes communicate via other paths

8. Step 1 – Address bus set up (with location to be written to)

   Step 3 – write (control) line is activated

9. *Any one from:*
   - Identifies the data to be used by/passed into and out of subroutines/subprocesses/procedures/functions
   - Data flow identifies parameters (order, type, value, reference, IN, OUT, IN/OUT)

10. TrueBasic: LET physicsTerm$ = firstTerm$ & secondTerm$
    Visual Basic: physicsTerm = firstTerm & secondTerm
    Java: physicsTerm: = firstTerm + secondTerm
    LiveCode: PUT firstTerm & secondTerm INTO physicsTerm
    (or any other valid syntax)

11. - The scope of a global variable is the entire program.
    - The scope of a local variable is one subroutine.

12. *Any two from:*
    - stores list of values
    - each element has the same data type
    - uses a single identifier
    - uses indexing
    - has fixed number of elements

13. *Any two from:*
    - Allows new functions to be added to existing software.
    - Enables the automation of complex/repeated operations.
    - Allows customisation of interface/menus/package.
    - Allows access to low level functions.

14. *Any one from:*
    - ITG has no bias (towards the client group or the software house) during testing.
    - The developers may be reluctant to choose test data which highlights shortfalls in their own work, unlike the ITG.

15. - The program will work on computer systems other than the one it was designed on/using alternative OS.
    - with little or no change.

16. *Any one from:*
    - The purpose of the subroutine
    - The required list of parameters
    - The order of the parameters
    - Each parameter type
    - Data flow

17. - Perfective
    - This is a new requirement from the client/not in the original specification.

SECTION II

18. (*a*) *Any two from:*
    - Small physical size
    - Large (data storage) capacity
    - Low power requirements
    - Fast access times

    (*b*) - Data format conversion – converting temperature signals eg analogue to digital/serial to parallel
    - Buffering – temporary storage of data in transit between the component and the computer/compensates for differences in speed
    - Handling of status signals – to ensure data from sensors are received correctly
    - Voltage conversion – to change voltage level of sensor to relevant value for computer
    - Protocol conversion – to ensure sensor and computer adhere to the same protocols

    (*c*) 1 picture = 4 * 6 * 1024 * 1024 * 24 bits

    603979776 bits = 72 Megabytes
    12 Gigabytes = 1024 * 12 Megabytes

    Max no. pictures = (1024 * 12)/72 = 170 pictures

    (*d*) - Input/Output (management) – coordinate transfer of blocks of data/check if devices ready for data transfer/detect transmission errors/buffer data transit
    - File management – update FAT/locate location of data blocks for storing (updating) file/protect existing files from being overwritten
    - Memory management – to hold the address/location of the uploaded data whilst it is in main memory/protect existing data from being overwritten
    - Resource allocation – ensure processor time and memory are allocated to the process
    - Interpreting user instructions – receive user commands to backup data
    - Error reporting – report any problems encountered during the process

    (*e*) Copyright, Designs & Patents Act

19. (*a*) Data bus width is incorrect
    Any one of following
    - 8 bit small for modern computer (likely 64–128 bit)
    - 8 bit gives 35 bit address bus
    - 8 bytes, not bits
    - Other valid

(b) $2^{AB} * 8 = 34359738368$
so $2^{AB} = 4294967296 = 2^{32}$,
Address bus width = 32bits
or
$2^{AB} * 8 = 32$ Gigabytes
$2^{AB} = 32 * 2^{30}/8 = 4 * 2^{30} = 2^{32}$
Address bus width = 32 bits
or
$2^{AB} = 32$ Gb/64bits
$2^{AB} = 4294967296$
Address bus width = 32 bits

(c) *Any one from:*
- Cache has faster access time than main memory /shortens fetch time
- Holds frequently used instructions/short fetch time
- Wider internal bus therefore faster transfer
- Cache is on the processor/shorter fetch time (faster transfer)

(d) *Any two from:*
- Application based tests measure performance in real-life tasks
- Take account of the whole system
- Are more independent of architecture
- and therefore give a more realistic view of performance

(e) *Any one from:*
- Security of data/access harder to control without a centralised server
- Centralised storage of data needed to allow users access from varying machines
- Cannot perform centralised backup easily since data is stored on different systems
- Large number of peers would lead to problems with backup/hard to locate distributed files
- Different levels of access required harder to set up in peer-to-peer (through shared folders)

(f) *Any one from:*
- Data sent to a single node with switch hub broadcasts to all nodes
- Each connected node on a switch receives full bandwidth nodes on a hub share the bandwidth
- Hub broadcasts increasing traffic point-to-point switch leading to reduced chance of collisions

(g) *Any two from:*
- disk editor
- disk cleanup
- disk defragmenter
- compression software
- firewall
- any other valid

20. (a) *Any two from:*
- Observe/shadow a pupil/teacher as they go from class to class and take notes on their activities.
- Look at any current materials/course documents used by class teachers.
- Interview staff and/or pupils.
- Use questionnaires.

(b) *Any two from:*
- To act as part of a legally binding contract between the client and the developers.
- To act as the main guide to the remaining stages of the software development process.
- To <u>identify exactly/detail/specify precisely</u> what new maths software will do.
- Identify scope and boundaries of problem.
- Validate final program against software specification.
- Any other valid response.

(c) *Any one from:*
Flow chart, structure diagram/chart, semantic net, etc

(d) Top down breaks down problem into simpler steps
Stepwise refinement continues this process until coding becomes trivial.

(e) *Any one from:*
- The nature of the problem to be solved
- Type of language (event-driven, etc)
- Type of user interface
- Type of hardware/OS
- The current skills of the programming team
- Features of the language (data types/functions/etc)
- Portability of language
- Any other valid

(f) Brief description of test/document/process that evidences (*any two from*):
- Speed of execution/use of the processor
- Amount of RAM/memory used
- Use of cache memory/registers/disk accesses
- Benchmarking tests
- efficient use of loops/data structures/parameters/etc or examples of these

21. (a) CASE price
when <= 500 then
    discountRate = 10
when < 1000 then
    discountRate = 12
when >= 1000 then
    discountRate = 15
End CASE

(b) An array of Booleans/strings

(c) *Any two from:*
- Uses a stored set/list of facts and rules (about music and mood)
- Pattern matching used to apply these rules to user's mood
- Queries can be used (to interrogate the knowledge base)
- Justification facility might explain music choice
- Lists can be processed
- Any other valid.

(d) *Any one from:*
- The order that program code is executed is dependent on which check boxes the user selects
- Code is attached to on-screen objects (such as buttons) which are selected by the user
- Code blocks are activated by user actions (such as clicking on buttons)
- Any other valid

(e) *Any two from:*
- If maintenance is required, code would need to be re-entered from listing or the machine code edited.
- No test record for the program will make maintenance more difficult.
- No user guide may cause problems for novice users.
- No technical guide may cause installation problems.
- Many other valid answers are possible.

22. (a) (i) Fastest = HorseTimes(1)

Loop from 2 to 5

If HorseTimes (current) < Fastest then
Set Fastest = HorseTimes (current)
End of if statement
Return to start of loop

(ii) • Change the < sign to > (can also accept > =).
  • Change the initialisation value if appropriate eg slowest = 0.

(iii) Counting occurrences.

(b) *Any two from:*
  • A compiler will translate the contents of a loop only once.
  • An interpreter will translate the contents of a loop every time it repeats.
  • A compiler does not use processor time retranslating.

(c) (i) *Any one from:*
  • Systematic testing will test each subroutine, subsystem and then the whole system independently
  • Testing will take place in a logical/ordered/planned way **or** following an agreed plan

(ii) *Any one from:*
  • Comprehensive testing will use normal, extreme and exceptional test cases
  • Test the full range of inputs/across all combinations

SECTION III PART A: ARTIFICIAL INTELLIGENCE

23. (a) *Any one from:*
  • Cannot go on forever – rules do not allow it
  • Clearly defined rules/moves
  • Clearly define start and end conditions
  • No element of chance
  • Closed world
  • Limited/restricted domain
  • You have complete information – no aspects of the game are hidden unlike many other games
  • It can be expanded using search trees because all possible moves can be evaluated
  • Any other reasonable

(b) (i) The ability of a <u>machine</u> to do things thought to require intelligence when done by people

(ii) *Any one from:*
  • Chess computer is problem solving – an aspect of intelligence
  • Chess computer can beat people that have intelligence so must be intelligent
  • Chess computer would know if board is set up wrongly
  • Demonstrate other aspects of intelligence – learn/cognitive ability/recall
  • Any other suitable

(iii) *Any one from:*
  • Chess computer has no actual understanding of the game or the situation
  • Chess computer is an example of a machine displaying the programmer's intelligence
  • Chess computer cannot learn
  • Limited aspects of intelligence are involved

(c) After a few moves the number of nodes will grow massively /few moves ahead will have a huge number of nodes when/evaluating a small number of nodes ahead e.g. 6 moves = 206 = 64 000 000

(d) (i) Heuristic

(ii) • Reduces search time by not evaluating/examining/ expanding poor moves (and their evaluation functions)/by expanding better moves

  • Reduces search space by not evaluating/ examining/expanding poor moves (and their evaluation functions)/by expanding better moves

24. (a) (i) Semantic net

(ii) • Each line represents a fact.
  • Each line informs/decides the predicate.
  • The nodes inform/decide the arguments of a Prolog fact.
  • The arrow direction decides the order of the arguments.

(b) (i) • have(spiders, eight_legs)
  • have(spiders, silk)
  • are(black_widow, spiders)
  • any other suitable

(ii) have(X,Y):- are(X,Z) , have(Z,Y)
  Accept :
  have(X,eight_legs):- are(X,spider) , have(spider, eight_legs)
  or
  have(X,eight_legs):- are(X,Z) , have(Z, eight_legs)

(iii) *Any one from:*
  • Reduces the need for stating multiple/numerous/additional facts.
  • Allows all members of a group to have the same attributes without having to write each out.

25. (a) (8, 8, 8)

(b) (i) (8,10,6) and (11,7,6)

(ii) • (2,19,3) AND THEN ONE OF (4,17,3) or (2,16,6) or (4,19,1)
  • (1,17,6) AND THEN ONE OF (1,11,12) or (2,16,6) or (2,17,5)
  • (2,20,2) AND THEN ONE OF (4,18,2) or (2,18,4)

(iii) • Breadth-first will find optimal solution to the puzzle (shortest solution will be found first)
  • Depth-first may expand a large number of nodes down the left side without finding a solution.
  • Avoids being stuck in an infinite loop by repeating aset of nodes.

(c) Moves can be evaluated independently by multiple processors at the same time.

26. (a) A=blaven B=928
  Must have A= , B=

(b) Matches at 5, <u>sub-goal munro(A, ,P)</u>
  Matches at 1, A instantiates benmacdhui, P to 1309, <u>new sub_goal munro(B, , R)</u>
  Matches at 1, B instantiates benmacdhui, R to 1309, new <u>sub_goal 1309>1309 fails</u>
  <u>Backtracks to line 1/line 2</u> , match at 2, instantiates B=cairntoul, R to 1291, <u>new sub_goal 1309>1291 succeeds</u>
  <u>Outputs A=benmacdhui B=cairntoul</u>

(c) • variable temporarily adopts a value (which is true)
  • variable adopts a current value
  • instance of a variable (which is currently true)

27. (a) (i) Knowledge base

(ii) • Why a question is being asked.
  • How a conclusion is reached.

(iii) *Any one from:*
  • User confidence in advice.
  • Testing the expert system.
  • Any other suitable

(b) (i) Subject area is restricted to a small area of knowledge eg respiratory compared to medicine.

(ii) *Any one from:*
- Restricted number of facts/rules
- Faster development time
- Processing/memory requirements are reduced.

(iii) • Lack of common sense
- Level of expertise required to set up/maintain
- Inability to learn/acquire new knowledge
- Inflexibility
- Lack of empathy/human can empathise

(c) (i) Corrective

(ii) • Language/terminology of the domain will be difficult causing difficulty when altering rules
- Expert would have difficulty with the formulation/expression of their own knowledge causing difficulty when formulating rules
- Difficulty when testing by having to check output with a human expert
- Both domain expert and knowledge engineer expertise are required when performing maintenance.

28. (a) (i) *Any two from:*
- Sound split into phonemes/blocks
- Phonemes/blocks pattern matched against stored sounds/patterns
- Words are identified from the phoneme/blocks

(ii) • The phonemes/sounds are the same/very similar for "mature" "much" "your" (or similar example)

(b) There is ambiguity in the sentence such as,
- Charges as a noun has different meanings
- Charges can be a noun and a verb
- Dropped as a verb has more than one meaning
- Submarine attack or attacked.

(c) Speech synthesis

(d) • NL searching,
- NL database interfaces,
- speech driven software
- chatterbots

SECTION III PART B: COMPUTER NETWORKING

29. (a) *Any two from:*
- Allocate different levels of user right/Ensure file & folder permissions are set correctly/Allow access only to appropriate areas
- Encrypt all data/Ensure that data is not intercepted during transmission
- Use of a Firewall
- Use a secure protocol such as HTTPS
- Use Packet Switching to transfer data
- Use a "call back" facility
- Any other valid

(b) (i) *Any two from:*
- There is a direct connection/dedicated channel between two devices
- Established for the duration of transmission
- All data follows the same physical path

(ii) *Any one from:*
- Packet switching usually faster than circuit as it allows network hardware to decide on most efficient/fastest route
- Communication channels can be shared since packets from different users can be mixed along a transmission line
- Security may be improved because if line is "hacked" only individual packets will be intercepted rather than whole message/file

(iii) *Any two from:*
- Check for simultaneous transmission/line is free
- Check to see if a collision is detected
- Make nodes wait a random amount of time
- Re-transmits after a collision
- Allows many users to access network at the same time

(c) (i) • TCP splits the file into packets
- TCP adds a header
- TCP reassembles the packets when they arrive at their destination address

(ii) • IP adds its own address header to each packet.
- IP routes the packets around the network.

(iii) *Any one from:*
- http
- FTP

(d) *Any one from:*
- The <u>firewall prevented</u> access to the network
- Examples of firewall, eg: IP address blocking, blocking of ports
- Wrong access rights allocated/set
- Incorrect recording/entry/typing of username/password

(e) *Any one from:*
- No closing card tag
- </card> missing

30. (a) (i) Spider or Crawler Based Search Engine

(ii) Meta-Search Engine

(b) *Any two from:*
- Accesses a database of valid domain names/URLs
- Translates the I-Play domain name/URL into its IP address
- Returns correct IP address of the I-Play website to the machine requesting the website

(c) *Any one from:*
- Games are immediately available to the customer
- Less manufacturing costs
- No postage costs
- Don't get lost in post
- Patches/upgrades are available instantly
- Any other valid

(d) Rate = Size/time
- Size = 200 × 8 = 1600 Megabits
- Rate = 1600/(3 * 60) = 8.9 Mbps

(e) *Any one from:*
- Players might be intimidated with face-to-face contact with people but find the anonymity of a website "safe"
- Collaboration with other players may be a prerequisite for making progress in a game hence players are encouraged to interact with other people
- Social interaction is required for playing multiplayer games and encourages friendships with other players
- Increased accessibility to other players online by encouraging communication as part of the game
- Any other valid

(f) *Any one from:*
- Use Anti-Virus Software – used to help to protect a network against virus threats.
- Firewall – analyse data coming into network to prevent denial of service attack
- Use of fault tolerance components – duplicating hardware components so that if a piece of hardware fails, you will have another sitting waiting to take its place.
- Use of uninterrupted power supplies – supplies enough electricity to a server to keep it going during a power cut.

- Regular maintenance – Using good quality components and having regular maintenance checks can help to avoid failure of hardware components.

(g) (i) *Any one from:*
- Data could be intercepted (while being transmitted and copied)
- Monitoring of data transmission
- Any other valid

(ii) *Any one from:*
- Changing/deleting data on the network
- Deliberately bringing down the network/Denial Of Service Attack
- Modification of the data stream/Creation of a false stream/generates false information
- Any other valid

(iii) *Any one from:*
- A passive attack does not involve any alteration/changing of the data
- No changes would be monitored by the software
- Any other valid

(h) *Any one from:*
- Devices are too far apart
- Interference from other devices/atmospheric interference
- Any other valid

(i) *Any two from:*
- ADSL will provide faster access to the website/have higher bandwidth than ISDN
- More multimedia content can be transmitted

31. (a) (i) Presentation

(ii) Network

(b) Class B
As this allows 65,534 devices to be networked/has sufficient addresses

(c) (i) *Any one from:*
- Bandwidth consumption This degrades the network performance by sending a large number of data packets in a short period of time
- Resource starvation An attack which is intended to use resources that would bring the network down
- Programming flaws This takes advantage of bugs in networking software
- Attacking the routers This involves "hi-jacking" data packets and routing them to the target server, which then gets flooded with data packets, or re-directing them to false addresses
- Domain Name Server attacks This involves sending a large number of DNS queries with a spoofed IP address of the target server

(ii)
- System resources are taken up by the attempted attack which prevents normal use of the network
- The former employee would know where weaknesses are in the network and therefore have the knowledge to be able to bypass security
- Correctly formed packets are not picked up by the firewall or anti-virus and these packets are then "flooded" onto the network

(d) *Any two from:*
Allow them to...
- monitor e-mails
- monitor telephone calls
- check Internet history
- access decryption keys/encrypted data
- undertake undercover surveillance
- Any other valid

(e)
- <center> <b> Tax Calculator </b></center>
- <div align=center> <b> Tax Calculator </b></div>
- <p align="center"> <b>Tax Calculator </b></p>

(f) *Any one from:*
- Small file size due to JPEG files being compressed
- Fast download times due to small file size/JPEG files being compressed
- JPEG supports millions of colours/has large bit depth/24 bit to allow a more realistic/better quality image
- Standard file format allowing the image to be opened by many programs

SECTION III PART C: MULTIMEDIA TECHNOLOGY

32. (a) (i) Storyboard

(ii) *Any one from:*
- Details each of the multimedia objects (and their attributes)
- Details navigation structure
- Details user interface

(b) *Any one from:*
- Do not need different viewers/players
- Do not have to learn authoring code (HTML etc) to create slides
- Any other valid

(c) *Any two from:*
- To allow hardware decoding of files
- To add effects
- Synchronise channels for sound
- Allow compress/decompress
- Any other valid

(d) (i) The note would play for longer

(ii) The sound would play at a faster speed

(e) Normalisation

(f)
- Embed files – all graphics etc are included in the presentation file
- Container file – allows different component files to be stored as a single file

33. (a) *Any two from:*
- SVG is a vector graphic file format
- allows logo to be resized with no loss of quality
- as it is resolution independent
- logo includes few objects so file size likely to be small

(b) Image B
GIF supports transparency/opacity (JPEG does not)

(c) *Any two from:*
- image starts to appear in stages
- Low resolution appears first
- subsequently refined to display complete/full image

(d) (i) *Any two from:*
- Combination of pixels of different colours
- Dithering is used to give the illusion of colours/
- shades in an image
- not in the palette

(ii) GIF only supports 256 colours/is 8 bit

(e) (i) *Any one from:*
- To define the available colours for the file
- To attempt/allow the consistent display of colours

(ii) *Any one from:*
- Allows customisations of colour set
- change to CLUT/palette affects entire graphic at once (rather than editing individual pixels)
- Restricts the bit depth to restrict the file size

(f) (i) • Repeated pixels of the same colour
- are stored using colour code of 1 pixel followed by the number of repeats

(ii) *Any two from:*
- Patterns/sequences of pixels are stored in a dictionary/table
- Pointers are used to reference the dictionary/table
- Shorter code replaces larger patterns of pixels

(g) (i) The numbers indicate the mix of colours (red, green and blue) (needed to represent a colour)

(ii) The colour would become more blue

(iii) 2^{24} or $2^8 \times 2^8 \times 2^8$ or $256 \times 256 \times 256$ or 16777216

34. (a) File size=60 Mb = $60 \times 8 \times 1024 \times 1024$ bits=503316480 bits
Sample size=(Sampling freqxSampling depthxChannels)
Time = File size/sample size
= $503316480/(88200 \times 24 \times 2)$
= 503316480/4233600
= 118.88… s
= 119 s

(b) *Any one from:*
- Don't have to connect to a computer to transfer data
- Infinite memory available(use of large/multiple cards)
- Can change card when full

(c) *Any two from:*
- Natural sound is analogue
- needs converted to digital before processing
- by digital computer

(d) WAV has more natural/better quality sound
- MP3 uses lossy compression
- WAV uses lossless compression

(e) *Any two from:*
- Recordings are 2 track/channel
- System detects stereo (so only uses 2 channels)
- Speakers are poorly positioned so losing their effect

(f) (i) *Any two from:*
- No cable/it is wireless/both phones have WiFi
- Fast transfer rate
- Large range

(ii) Bluetooth
- connection is <u>direct</u> between devices
- short range required
- both will have Bluetooth (if they have WiFi)
- other valid with justification

(g) No. of frames = $60 \times 15 = 900$
File size = No. of frames x No of pixels x bit depth
= $900 \times 640 \times 360 \times 2$ bytes (1)
= 414720000 bytes = 405000 Kb =
395.5078125Mb
= 396 Mb

35. (a) • A simple image containing few objects/shapes
- Use a simple logo
- Accept valid example

(b) Has to be converted to a bit map (before rendering)

(c) *Any one from:*
- A 2D bitmap image mapped onto surface of 3D object (to give the impression of roughness/smoothness)
- The application of a type of surface to a 3D image.

(d) *Any one from:*
- Depth/z coordinate
- Shadow
- Angle of rotation
- Any other valid

(e) *Any one from:*
- VRML
- WRL
- X3D

COMPUTING HIGHER 2014

SECTION I

1. −50

2. *Any one from:*
   - Unicode can represent a wider range of characters (sets) than ASCII
   - Unicode uses 16 bits per character allowing for representation of more character sets
   - Unicode allows for user-defined characters whereas ASCII does not

3. *Any two from:*
   - Start X / X1
   - Start Y / Y1
   - Finish X / X2
   - Finish Y / Y2
   - (Line) thickness/stroke-width
   - (Line) colour
   - (Line) pattern
   - Any other valid

4. *Any one from:*
   - Hold data (to be processed)
   - Hold an address (to be accessed)
   - Any other valid

5. Addressability

6. *Any two from:*
   - Access/write/read times/speeds are faster (than magnetic devices)
   - Device can be smaller in physical size (without constraints of space for moving parts)
   - Fragmentation does not result in greater seek time
   - Less power is required for solid state drives (as moving parts within hard drives require more power)
   - Actual data transfer rate will be higher due to architecture of SSD

7. Data format conversion

8. *Any one from:*
   - Store/process webpages
   - Allows access to web pages (HTML pages)/HTTP documents
   - Allows website hosting
   - Allows server side creation of dynamic webpages
   - Caching frequently accessed webpages
   - Filtering content of incoming data/webpages
   - Any other valid

9. *Any one from:*
   - To instigate system start-up
   - Load start-up instructions to RAM
   - Locate/Load OS on backing storage/in boot sector
   - Locate system folder on hard disk drive/solid state drive

10. Utility Software/Utility Program/Utilities

11. (a) *Macro Virus*

    (b) *Any two from:*
    - An initial checksum/calculation is performed on the file (prior to infection)
    - A second checksum/calculation is performed upon opening/execution
    - A difference in the value returned indicates the possible presence of a virus

12. Discussions / interviews / meetings between analyst & client will be repeated
    AND one of:
    - To clarify exact requirements
    - As a result of new information
    - To confirm budgets (timescales)
    Or
    Repeated refinement of specification based on new information

13. (a) Pseudocode

    (b) *Any one from:*
    - In: amount
    - In: rate
    - Out: interest

14. *Any two from:*
    - Code is prewritten/so does not need to be typed in
    - Code is pretested/error free/so less time required during testing
    - Code is pre-documented/so less time required during documentation stage
    - Programmer can use code which he/she may not have been able to produce himself/herself

15. (a) Efficiency / efficient

    (b) Portability / portable

16. *Any one from:*
    - (To allow experts) to extend / customise the functionality of the application
    - To make the application more flexible / usable by a larger group of users/novice users
    - Customise the user interface
    - Increase productivity due to macros executing faster than human/manual execution/automate repetitive tasks
    - Allows complex actions to be triggered by one key press

17. (a) *Any two from:*
    - Data type
    - Number of elements / size of array/ range of indices/index number
    - Initial value
    - Position in RAM
    - Any other valid

    (b) • Does not take up additional memory/contains only the memory address pointer storing a second copy of the array
      Or
    - Does not waste processor time making a second copy of the array

18. *Any two from:*
    - Test the program more objectively/without bias/no expectation of output
    - More likely to apply a range of test data/cases
    - ITG are likely to find errors missed by programmers during testing/avoids corrective maintenance
    - ITG will not sign off the project just to make a deadline

SECTION II

19. (a) (i) *Any one from:*
       - Pixel Level Editing
       - Michael could include photographs
       - Not limited to mathematical objects

    (ii) *Any one from:*
       - Resolution independent
       - Scalable without losing detail/becoming blocky
       - Layering (of objects) is possible
       - Edit individual objects rather than pixel–by–pixel
       - Any other valid

(b) • Temporarily stores print jobs in (fast) backing storage (accept an example)
• Queues jobs until printer is ready to receive them

(c) *Any two from:*
• Enough available/minimum necessary backing storage to store the software
• Enough main memory/RAM to allow the software to run
• Adequate clock speed to process data
• Compatibility of processor
• Availability of appropriate peripherals/interfaces/sound card/graphics card

(d) *Any two from:*
• Locates data in main memory prior to transfer
• Communicates with file management (to ensure that the file allocation table is updated)
• Communicates with I/O Management (to ensure that data can be transferred to backing storage)

(e) Copyright, Designs and Patents Act

20. (a)

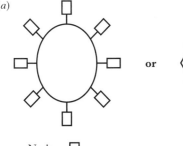 **or**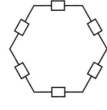

Node

Channel ———

(b) *Any two from:*
• Busy
• Clear to send/Ready to send
• Request to send
• Acknowledge
• Synchronise
• Clear to receive/Ready to receive
• Any other valid

(c) *Any one from:*
• Fewer transmission errors as skewing is not an issue.
• Single line ensures that data cannot be skewed

(d) Watching, as the virus is watching for a specific action/condition (the online bank access)

(e) • Worms self-replicate (without a host), a Trojan horse cannot self-replicate
or
• Worms replicate across networks attacking ports, a Trojan horse will only infect one station at a time

21. (a) • Pre-fetched instructions stored in cache, reducing time needed to access slower main memory
or
• Holds frequently used instructions (preloaded into cache) speeding up the fetch/execute cycle
or
• Cache memory switching/access speed is high reducing latency/idle time

(b) 1 Set address bus up with relevant memory address
2 Data bus is set up with data to be written/transferred
3 Write line is activated
4 Data on data bus is transferred to memory location identified by address bus

(c) Possible solutions:

$2^{32} * d = 64GB$ $64Gb/2^{32} =$ data bus width 549755813888/4294967296 bits = 128	64GB = 549755813888 bits $2^{32} = 4294967296$ memory locations 549755813888/4294967296 = 128	$2^{32} = 4GB$ 64/4 = 16 Bytes 16*8 = 128
Data Bus Width is 128 (lines)	**Data Bus Width is 128 (lines)**	**Data Bus Width is 128 (lines)**

(d) *Any two from:*
(i) • FLOPS isolate processor capability/are independent of other components when measuring performance
• FLOPS are independent of instruction size
• FLOPS are independent of instruction complexity
• FLOPS are independent of word size
• FLOPS are independent of clock speed
• FLOPS are a measure of actual arithmetic capability
• FLOPS provide an industry standard for measuring processor performance

(ii) Application based tests take account of other aspects of the system (such as main memory/cache memory/data bus width)

22. (a) *Any two from:*
• Unwillingness of some members of staff to cooperate leading to lack of information
• Contradictory information given
• Irrelevant information given
• Inaccurate/Incomplete information given
• Lack of knowledge in relation to how the current system could be improved
• Any other valid

(b) The problem is broken down into smaller / easier to solve (sub) problems

(c) *Any two from:*
• Pre-defined routines for the creation of objects
• Pre-defined code attached to each object
• Order of execution is decided by the user (does not follow a specific order)
• Allow sections of code to be triggered/executed via a button

(d) • Programmers will each be writing individual subprograms for software required
• Thus reducing implementation time
or
• They must collaborate via meetings/project manager/detailed plan
• Will discuss how to implement the design/get help from more experienced programmer
or
• Discuss testing to reduce time wasted/find and solve problems earlier
• Ensure testing is systematic and comprehensive
or
• Programmers will each be writing individual subprograms for software required
• They must collaborate via meetings/project manager/detailed plan

(e) *Any one from:*
• Methodical / Logical / planned checking of software.
• Test individual subroutines, then modules, up to whole system testing

(f) *Any one from:*
- More memory efficient as translator software not held in memory
- More processor efficient as program not translated each time the program runs
- Source code unavailable therefore protected from alteration/editing/copyright infringement
- Any other valid reason with appropriate explanation

(g) *Any two from:*
- Descriptive variable/procedure names
- Effective use of whitespace (indentation and/or blank lines)
- Internal commentary
- Use of functions/subroutines/modules
- Any other valid

(h) *Any two from:*
- To make the software accessible to more users/platforms/operating systems (increase sales)
- Reduced workload for implementation on new platforms
- Reduced workload for future upgrades
- Any other valid

(i) Perfective as they are adding a new feature not in the original software

23. (a) Joining together of (sub) strings/characters

(b) Array of strings

(c) (i) Set count to zero
　　For each member
　　　　If region(position) = "East" OR region(position) = "West" then
　　　　　　Add 1 to count
　　　　End if
　　End loop

　　or

　　Counter=0
　　For member= 1 to number
　　　　If region(member) = "East" OR region(member) = "West" then
　　　　　　counter=counter + 1
　　　　End if
　　Next member

(ii) If region(position) = "East" OR region(position) = "West"
　　　Add 1 to count
　　　Display email(position)
　　End if

(iii) *Any one from:*
- CASE (statement)
- Nested IF

(d) (i) Whole program

(ii) *Any two from:*
- Makes data flow clearer, so improves maintainability / readability
- Increases portability, can re-use without changing variable names
- Aids modularity
- Reduces unexpected clashes between variable names
- Reduces impact or load on main memory
- Any other valid

SECTION III PART A: ARTIFICIAL INTELLIGENCE

24. (a) *Any three from:*
- Identify keywords from Niall's input
- Match keywords to a standard set of phrases and output
- Or manipulate the sentence structure to create a new phrase
- Respond generically if no match found
- Any other valid

(b) *Any one from:*
- No effect, since keywords are irrelevant of order
- No effect, since any keywords will still be identified and the matching response output
- No effect, since it responds generically
- Won't be able to parse/analyse/determine the meaning of the sentence so will output generic response

(c) (i) NLU – Natural Language Understanding
　　AND
- Attempts to derive meaning of the sentence
　　or
- parses sentence to identify components /nouns/verbs etc
　　or
- identifies the meaning of words
　　or
- Any other valid

(ii) NLG – natural language generation

(d) *Any one from:*
- Changing nature of language – google. surf etc
- Ambiguity such as multiple meanings – saw, charge
- Incorrect use of words with different spelling – sea instead of see

(e) *Any one from:*
- Use of humour because computers would deal literally instead of recognising humour
- Referring back to previous responses because computers would not be able to store or track previous responses
- Use current/topical knowledge because up-to-date knowledge may not be coded.
- Use non-standard language/slang
- Any other valid

(f) *Any two from:*
- Procedural uses a range of data types for variables
- Procedural uses control structures such as loops etc
- Sequence of statements is more rigid in a procedural language/defined start and end
- Procedural follows a programmer designed algorithm
- Any other valid

25. (a) *Any two from:*
- Specialise in a particular field of medicine
- Specialise in a particular age group, gender etc
- Any other valid

(b) *Any one from:*
- The outputs from one layer of neurons are fed to the next layer as input
- Each neuron takes inputs from others on the layer below.
- Any other valid

(c) (i) *Any two from:*
- Expected output and actual output are different
- Weights are altered/rebalanced to reduce or increase the influence of an input
- Influences when the neuron fires (as a result of exceeding the threshold value)
- To achieve the desired output

Any one from:

(ii) • Threshold value
 • Level/value at which a neuron is fired

(iii) The process of feeding inputs and known outputs is repeated until correct results produced

(d) *Any two from:*
 • Multiple processors
 • Can perform multiple neuron calculations at the same time
 • Reducing response times for diagnosis

(e) *Any two from:*
 • Problem solving
 • Memory
 • Creativity
 • Cognitive ability
 • Language

26. (a) [( ), ( ), (3,2,1)]

(b)

Start state	X	Y
[(3,2,1), ( ), ()]	[(3,2), (1), ()]	[(3), (1), (2)] or [(3,2), ( ), (1)]
[(3,2,1), ( ), ()]	[(3,2), ( ), (1)]	[(3), (2), (1)] or [(3,2), (1), ()]

(c) Uses less memory
 AND
 • Because it only holds nodes on the current path
 or
 • Can backtrack and so can abandon nodes/remove nodes/overwrite nodes

(d) (i)

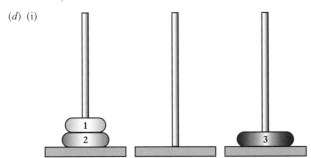

(ii) • [(2),(1),(3)]
 • [( ),(1),(3,2)]

(e) (i) *Any two from:*
 • Each descendant node is scored
 • Locating the more promising/likely node or discarding less likely nodes
 • Reducing the search space/nodes to be calculated or considered

(ii) • Each node can only have few/ two or three descendants
 • Which means that the search tree / amount of nodes will not become large (within a small number of moves)

(iii) *Any one from:*
 • Use of cache or larger cache
 • Increased clock speed
 • Larger RAM / faster access RAM
 • Any other valid

27. (a) A=eardrum, A=ossicles

(b) ?- function_of(A, cerebellum).

(c) • Match at 13, A instantiated to ossicles, sub-goal is_part(ossicles,B)
 • Match at 8, B instantiated to middle_ear, output solution B=middle_ear
 • Match at 14, A instantiated to ossicles, sub-goal is_part(ossicles,C)
 • Match at 8, C instantiated to middle_ear, sub-goal is located_in(middle_ear, B)
 • Match at 13, A instantiated to middle_ear, sub-goal is_part(middle_ear, B)
 • Match at 2, B instantiated to ear, output B=ear

(d) *Any two from:*
 • When a sub-goal fails or when no more descendants
 • Prolog returns to an earlier point (of success or instantiation in a sub-goal)
 • Resumes searching from that point
 • Tries a previously untried branch

SECTION III PART B: COMPUTER NETWORKING

28. (a) (i) SMTP

(ii) FTP

(iii) HTTP

(b) Class B
 AND
 • The first octet (178) is in the correct range for class B (128 to 191)
 or
 • The position of the first zero in the binary conversion of the first octet is the second most significant bit

(c) *Any one from:*
 • The first two octets need to be the same as the others on the network (178.21)
 • The first octet should be the same as the others on the network/178

(d) *Any two from:*
 • The DNS searches its database for the domain name
 • Matches the Domain Name to its corresponding IP address
 • Returns the IP address to the browser

(e) • Open & close head tags in correct position
 • Open & close body tags in correct position
 • Open & close title tags in correct position (inside head tags) with correct text
 • Open & close underline tags with correct text as long as not located within the head or title tags

(f) (i) WAP (Wireless Application Protocol)

(ii) *Any one from:*
 • Code has been changed due to a change in the environment.
 • There are no new features being added or errors being corrected

(iii) *Any one from:*
 • WML has limited support for tables/images/ multimedia plugins
 • Pages arranged in stacks of cards in WML (A deck is a set of WML cards, a site is a set of HTML pages)
 • Limited text formatting/range of tags in WML
 • Restricted graphic format without conversion (to WBMP format)
 • Standard JPG/GIF/PNG formats cannot be displayed in WML without conversion (to WBMP format)
 • In WML, variables can be defined, (variables cannot be stored in HTML)

- WML is viewed in a micro-browser, (HTML uses regular browsers, such as Internet Explorer)
- WML is case sensitive, (HTML is not case sensitive)

(g) *Any two from:*
- The meta-search engine would send a request to multiple search engines
- The results would then be displayed in a single list
- Results in list will have been aggregated

(h) Spider
  To match the keywords returned by a user search

29. (a) Change Aimee's permissions/access rights to give access to the file

(b) *Any two from:*
- Any unauthorised change to data, for example a customer account
- Unauthorised transfer of money from one account to another
- Change the bank's network infrastructure configuration
- DOS attack/Resource Starvation to deliberately bring down the network
- Any other valid which indicates that data will be modified, destroyed, or redirected

(c) (i) • Data is sent one byte/character/group of bits at a time
     • A start and stop bit is used

   (ii) • The additional start & stop bits represent an extra overhead in the transmission process
     • And would increase data transfer time

(d) (i) *Any two from:*
     • TCP splits the data into packets
     • TCP adds a header/sequence number/header
     • TCP reassembles the packets when they arrive at their destination address

   (ii) *Any one from:*
     • IP adds its own <u>address</u> header to each packet
     • IP routes the packets around the network

(e) (i) *Any two from*
     • Block certain keywords
     • Block certain URLs/specific sites
     • Block certain/a range of IP addresses

   (ii) A walled garden has a list of suitable sites and only these can be accessed

   (iii) *Any one from:*
     • Some/new unsuitable URLs might not be on the restricted list
     • Some/new unsuitable keywords might not be on the restricted list
     • Use of a proxy server to bypass internet filtering software and access unsuitable sites

30. (a) (i) *Any two from:*
     • Each packet is given a destination address and a sequence number
     • Each individual packet can take a different path through the network to its destination
     • At the destination the packets are reassembled (using their sequence number)

   (ii) • Communication channels can be shared since packets from different users can be mixed along a transmission line
     or
     • Improves system performance, as packets do not have to follow same route / each packet takes the most efficient route
     or

- Security improved, because if line is "hacked" individual packets will be intercepted rather than whole message / file
  or
- Packet switching data transfer rate is usually faster than circuit, as it allows network hardware to decide on most efficient / fastest route
  or
- Packet switching uses full bandwidth whereas circuit switching can result in unused bandwidth

(b) *Any two from:*
- WPAN (generally) operates at a lower bandwidth/slower data transfer than a WLAN
- WPAN operates at shorter distances than WLAN
- WPAN uses less power than WLAN
- WLAN would require a router

(c) (i) *Any one from:*
     To ensure that:
     • Communications equipment and networking software would be compatible
     • Computers (on different networks) could communicate with each other

   (ii) To uniquely identify each device on the network

   (iii) Data Link Layer

(d) (i) Odd (Parity)
     AND
     • number of / three 1's before being sent indicates odd parity
     or
     • even number of / four 1's at destination with an error indicates odd parity

   (ii) Cyclic redundancy check

(e) • Size = 25 x 8 = 200 megabits
   • Rate = 200/5 = 40 megabits per second
     or
   • 25/5 = 5 megabytes per second
   • 5 megabytes = 5 * 8 = 40 megabits per second

(f) (i) *Any one from:*
     • Can compare prices easily
     • Discounts are usually given for buying online
     • Less queuing at the shops/high street travel agents/don't need to travel to shop
     • Any other valid

   (ii) *Any two from:*
     • Small padlock (at the foot of the browser)
     • https (in the address bar)
     • Any other valid

SECTION III PART C: MULTIMEDIA TECHNOLOGY

31. (a) (i) *Any one from:*
     • Ready made buttons, colour schemes, etc are provided
     • No need for coding
     • See output in real time
     • Easier to preview (in different browsers)
     • Any other valid

   (ii) *Any one from:*
     • Greater control of features/timings
     • Access to low level commands
     • Access to other applications
     • Re-use blocks of code
     • Automatic code completion
     • Code/Syntax highlighting
     • Any other valid

(b) Adaptive
   or
   Corrective

(c) *Any one from:*
   - No permanent copy of file stored on computer - so reduces opportunity for (illegal) copying
   - The media plays as the data is received rather than waiting for the entire file to download before playback

(d) *Any one from:*
   - Any position of video can be played immediately as entire video is available rather than only the buffered content/frames
   - Entire file must be downloaded before playback therefore no lag/buffering

(e) No. of frames = 32 x 25 = 800
   Frame size = 1280 x 720 x 24 bits = 22118400 bits

   File size = No. of frames x Frame size

   = 800 x 22118400 bits
   = 17694720000 bits
   = 2.0599365234375 Gb
   = <u>2.06 Gb</u>

(f) • Each key frame is stored as a JPEG (which is itself compressed)
   • Delta frames store changes between intermediate frames

(g) (i) MIDI

   (ii) *Any two from:*
      - MIDI stores attributes of the sound
      - Different sound cards will interpret attributes differently to play a sound
      - Different sound cards have different in-built sounds used to synthesise playback

32. *Any two from:*
(a) • Increase resolution
   • Pixels are smaller so curves are smoother
   • Enable Interpolation

(b) • Anti-aliasing
   • Use of intermediate shades between two main colours/beside edges

(c) (i) JPEG does not support transparency (resulting in white boxes blocking background)

   (ii) • GIF
       • PNG

(d) GIF

(e) • Digital camera CCDs are in an array/table/grid
   • Scanner CCDs are arranged in a line

(f) (i) *Any one from:*
      - Output quality matches hardware capability, reducing likelihood of pixelation
      - Only a single file is needed rather than several files therefore reducing overall backing storage requirements

   (ii) *Any one from:*
      - Need to convert vector graphics into bitmap for display
      - Some characters may be overly complex / difficult to describe as vectors
      - Very small, but complex, graphics have smaller file sizes as bitmaps
      - More detailed customisation of fonts
      - Any other valid

33. (a) *Any two from:*
   - Depth/Z co-ordinate
   - Direction/Rotation
   - Lighting/shadow
   - Texture

(b) *Any one from:*
   - VRML (Virtual Reality Modelling Language/ Virtual Reality Markup Language)
   - WRL (VRML world file extension)

(c) *Any two from:*
   - Increased RAM/main memory
   - Increased processor clock speed/throughput
   - Multicore/parallel processing
   - Increased availability of (real and virtual) 3D monitors
   - Improved graphics cards
   - Any other valid

(d) Data can be stored in layers/three dimensions

34. (a) File size = 48000 × 12 x 16 × 6 bits
   = 55296000 bits
   = 6912000 bytes
   = 6750 Kb
   = 6.591796875 Mb
   = 6.59 Mb

(b) *Any one from:*
   - Surround sound
   - DSP (Digital Signal Processing)
   - DAC (Digital to Analogue Conversion)

(c) • Surround sound allows better impression of movement/panning/exact positioning of sound
   • Appropriate example – car/aircraft/helicopter passing, position of explosion, etc

(d) *Any one from:*
   - The amount of data required to store 1 second of sound
   - The number of bits to transferred in 1 second
   - Throughput required for playback

(e) (i) *Any one from:*
      - To make use of the full dynamic range
      - Increase amplitude of quiet sounds and decrease amplitude of loud sounds
      - To bring the average or peak amplitude to a target level

   (ii) *Any one from:*
      - Scaling of loud sounds would also reduce quiet sounds so they cannot be heard
      - Scaling of quiet sounds may magnify/boost any background noise
      - Sound balance may be unnatural

(f) (i) *Any one from:*
      - Convenient that all necessary files/file types are stored together in a single file
      - Easier to transfer a single file rather than many files

   (ii) May need a program/codec/plugin to recreate separate files

(g) (i) To allow output (from computer) to speakers

   (ii) • Carries out signal enhancements (reverberation/chorus effects)/applies effects
       • Handles MIDI files

(h) (i) • Difference between samples is stored.
       • Compression level 1:4 (using 4 bits rather than 16 bits)

   (ii) Sounds masked by loud sounds are not stored